More Praise
A How-To Guide for Business Giving

"Give for Good shares a platform for all businesses to realize the tremendous value creation that occurs at the intersection of doing well and doing good. This comprehensive and practical approach serves as a framework for businesses to turn good intentions into focused, effective business philanthropy."
- Sarah Harris, Vice President and Founder, Incite

"Give for Good is an amazing resource for anyone interested in achieving philanthropic goals! Debbie and Sam share their wisdom, methods and tools in an easy-to-follow approach that every organization can apply. The benefits of giving back are well known and using G4G makes it easy to join the movement."
- Dave Angelow, Adjunct Professor
McCoy School of Business, Texas State University

"Business leaders would do well to allow Sam and Debbie be their guides to the world of philanthropy. Their extensive experience consulting with nonprofits, business leaders, and civic leaders alike gives them a unique insight into how strategic business giving can strengthen work teams and have a real impact on social issues at the same time. Give For Good makes an undeniable case for strategic business giving, and it lays out the steps businesses large and small should take to get there. I've interviewed and studied a number of businesses with formal giving plans, and even they could use this book to refine their strategies. Considering today's hyper-competitive business environment, Give for Good is a must-have for creating your competitive edge."
- Monica Maldonado Williams, Director, GivingCity Austin

"This work goes a long way toward advancing the field of corporate philanthropy and community engagement — a field which is rapidly growing and evolving and is in need of this kind of strategic guidance."
- Matt Kouri, CEO, Mission Capital

"Want to do giving Better — capital B — for business, for your cause or for your whole city? This is the book to organize you, improve your planning, and increase your impact. Clear and engaging. Classically Sam & Debbie."
- Drake Zimmerman, Registered Principal, JD CFA CFP CAP
Zimmerman & Armstrong Investment Advisors, Inc.

"It is imperative for businesses to implement a stakeholder-first mentality. A company's ability to 'give' touches on all of its most vital stakeholders: employees, vendors, clients, and community, and Give for Good provides a guide for businesses to do just this."

- Neil Goldman, CEO & Founder, Hotels for Hope

"It's not business as usual anymore. Consumers want to buy from businesses that generate social currency for the world. Millennials will make up 75 percent of the global workforce by 2025 and want to work at inspired businesses. Philanthropy is being reshaped by Millennials — and Give For Good is a tool to help companies prepare for the next generation through understanding the unprecedented power of Millennials as influencers who are shaping our future in a myriad of ways."

- Maggie Miller, Chief Troublemaker, Digital Union

"The challenges a community faces are ever increasing, so leaders and customers look at businesses' bottom line with a focus on more than just profits and loss — they now measure how you give back. In Give for Good, you'll learn what your business needs to be help make a difference in your community."

- Sly Majid, Chief Service Officer
Office of Austin Mayor Steve Adler

"Eighty percent of North America's economy is built on the backs of small and medium-sized businesses and for the most part their social capital is built through the relationships they have established by working the 'main streets' of America. Unfortunately, resources to help these businesses, whether they are privately held family enterprises or publicly traded companies, are lacking . . . until now. Give for Good: A How-To Guide for Business Giving, is a much needed resource for the sector: business leaders, marketing managers, philanthropy advisors, and corporate citizenship directors. As someone who has spent almost 20 years working with family businesses and small enterprises to become more strategic in their philanthropy and social objectives, I am so excited to have this book as a tool to share with my clients."

- Gena Rotstein, CEO, Dexterity Ventures Inc. Place2Give

Give for
GOOD

A How-To Guide

for

Business Giving

Debbie Johnson and Sam Woollard

PHILANTHROPY
PRESS

ISBN: 978-0-9863973-0-1 (paperback)
978-0-9863973-1-8 (Kindle)
978-0-9863973-2-5 (ePub)

Library of Congress Control Number: 2015932353

Printed in the United States of America

Layout: Marc Schwarz
             Think Write Communications

Cover design: PixBeeDesign
                http://pixbeedesign.com

**PHILANTHROPY
PRESS**

Published by Philanthropy Press
1200 Barton Creek Blvd. #7
Austin, Texas 78735
info@successfulgiving.com

Table of contents

List of illustrations

Acknowledgments

Debbie and Sam would like to thank those who inspired us as we ventured into writing this book:

- Tracy Gary and her book, *Inspired Philanthropy*, which helped ground us and provided us with great guidance;

- Jason Franklin and his work with Bolder Giving, which showed us that setting big bold goals can produce amazing results;

- The many businesses who so generously shared their good, bad, and ugly experiences with philanthropy;

- Our clients who have helped us to hone our message and create the right tools;

- The writers who came before us, Nogie King, Thom Singer, Patti De-Nucci, and Nancy Oelklaus who all graciously shared their wisdom;

- And finally, our husbands, Lamar and Jeff, who have supported us through this lengthy process as we have written and rewritten so that we could produce something of the highest value possible.

Introduction

"My father used to say, 'You can spend a lot of time making money. The tough time comes when you have to give it away. How to give something back, that's the tough part in life.'"

- Lee Iacocca, past President, Ford Motor Company and past Chairman, Chrysler Corporation

Debbie's story

Debbie Johnson grew up in a "Leave it to Beaver" household. Her father worked hard to provide for their large family and her mom stayed home to take care of the kids until Debbie, as the youngest, was old enough for her mom to feel comfortable going to work. So while not rich, they wanted for nothing essential. She was also raised in the Christian tradition that taught "To whom much is given, much is required." She always knew how blessed she was and how that obligated her to share with others and give back. Couple that with a strong sympathy gene and she naturally ended up with a soft heart.

Professionally, she spent essentially all her career in the business world which didn't provide much outlet for day-to-day philanthropy so she took advantage of opportunities to give back at her church and in the community to scratch that itch. But at one point, by virtue of her job title at AT&T, she was able to design and implement the company's community giving program and found it to be one of the most satisfying experiences on the job. This exposure fueled her fire for creating great experiences for both business and nonprofit partnerships. And shifting her attention from sales and marketing exploits to philanthropy consulting has allowed her to further travel this path.

Sam's story

In the 1970's, the British economy faltered. There were trade union strikes, an oil crisis, and many employees were put on a three-day work week. Sam Woollard grew up during this time with her family having just enough money to take care of the basics, and not a lot left over. Even though her family was struggling, they made her keenly aware that many others were worse off, and she should be grateful that, while there was not much in the way of financial resources, she was surrounded by loving and caring family members who all worked together to support each other.

There was one incident when she was about eight that had a profound effect on how she viewed the world. She was part of a teacher training program that paired students with aspiring teachers and her student teacher took her to see a documentary that showed children in England who were hungry. Having grown up in a home where food was always available, she was deeply impacted by learning that others were not so fortunate.

This led her on a path of trying to figure out how to make a difference in the world. After graduating with a degree in social work, she initially set out on a direct client service track but quickly learned that her strengths lay in administration and connecting different parts of the social services system. Throughout her 25 years of working in the social services sector, she became increasingly aware of the lack of connection and understanding between the business and nonprofit sectors and sought to figure out a way to connect the two.

The Successful Giving story

Following Debbie's move to Texas, Debbie and Sam each had been told by various people that they should meet and so, in 2010, they met at a local coffee shop and discussed their respective career paths. It quickly became apparent that they shared a passion for strategic philanthropy and they realized that their complementary skills could, in tandem, help businesses become more thoughtful and strategic as they gave back to the community.

Through both of their experiences they learned that there is often a gap between the nonprofit and for-profit sectors. There are language and expectation differences that can result in confusion, misunderstanding, and often disappointment. There can be different value systems and marketing needs that must be addressed, and there are often fundamentally different ways of working and communicating.

They formed Successful Giving, LLC to close this gap, help business philanthropy increase, create meaningful experiences for both businesses and nonprofits, and ensure nonprofits can succeed in meeting their missions.

Why this book?

According to Giving USA, in 2015, corporate giving was nearly $18.4 billion representing approximately 5% of overall financial giving in the U.S.[1] When we reviewed the available literature regarding businesses and philanthropy, we discovered that the majority of it is written for large businesses, many of whom have a community affairs person.

However, these large businesses (over 500 employees) represent a tiny minority (1%) of all businesses and small businesses employ about half of U.S. workers. Many small and medium sized businesses want to engage in the community but are often either overwhelmed by unsolicited requests, or they don't know how to get involved or focus their energy.

Debbie and Sam wanted to provide practical guidance and solutions for businesses that want to effectively engage in the community but don't necessarily have the bandwidth and time to employ someone to make these critical decisions.

Why now?

Over the last several years, more research and focus has been placed on business philanthropy. It has become clear that businesses have a variety of motivations and reasons for giving, including:

- Internal reasons to give:
  - Improve employee attraction and retention
  - Enhance employee skills

- External reasons to give:
    - o   Build brand and corporate image
    - o   Increase revenue and market share

- Moral reasons to give:
    - o   Improve the community
    - o   Feel good/altruism

We are also entering an era in which Millennials and Generation Z are becoming the majority of the workforce. These generations expect that their workplaces will be integrated into the community, and they look for positions that will create opportunities for them to participate in the community, both in volunteer and leadership roles. In order for businesses to compete for these talented young people and create a loyal workforce, it is imperative that they understand this dynamic and provide appropriate outlets for giving and volunteering.

Only 39% of Millennials said companies discussed cause work during the interview process. Those that did influenced Millennials by doing so; 55% of them who heard about cause work in the interview said the company's involvement with causes helped persuade them to take the job.[2]

What to expect

In this book, Debbie and Sam will share their model and tools for business philanthropic decision making, outline some key learnings, and share stories of other businesses that have walked this path and succeeded. The book is organized around their **GIVES** model, which provides a framework that can be used to identify what issues you want to address, determine the best role for your business to play, ascertain which organizations are a good fit for your philanthropy, and learn how to evaluate your effectiveness. Using this model will allow you to turn whatever your motivation is into a successful outcome.

The ensuing chapters will provide greater detail and practical applications designed to provide you with the guidance and support you need to meet your giving goals.

Below is an outline and copy of the GIVES model. The model is based on five key components that can be incorporated to create a successful, sustainable giving program:

The GIVES Model

GEAR UP: This initial phase focuses on determining what you want to change and how to discover and define your areas of focus.

 Identify: In this section, you will identify your role in the change, how you will make decisions, and what, how much, and how you will give.

 Vet: This section focuses on who you will give to and provides tools for screening the nonprofits who might receive your gifts.

 Evaluate: By the end of this section, you will have the knowledge and tools to create an evaluation plan for your philanthropic investment.

 Start Over: Giving is cyclical and once you have evaluated your success, you can determine if you want to continue with your strategy or identify new areas to explore.

As you become increasingly comfortable and proficient with the GIVES model, we hope you will give for *good* (helping the world become a better place to live) as well as give *for good* (investing in the community for the rest of your life)!

Why Give?

> "There can be little doubt that a certain amount of corporate philanthropy is simply good business and works for the long-term benefit of the investors."

> - John Mackey, co-CEO of Whole Foods

We believe businesses should give as much emphasis to their philanthropy planning as to their employees, their growth potential, and other areas of their business plan. The "Director Notes" report from The Conference Board says it this way: "In order to ensure the effectiveness of corporate philanthropy programs, executives should apply the same prudence to giving decisions that they do to other business activities."[3]

Bruce DeBoskey in the *Denver Post* (March 2015) reinforced this point, noting "Successful companies now recognize that philanthropy is a key component of corporate citizenship and overall business strategy. Too often, corporate philanthropy is random and uncoordinated. To be truly effective, it must be strategic."[4]

However, as an initial part of the planning, it is important for businesses to understand the motivations for giving as each one has its own unique reasons for participating in philanthropy.

The virtuous cycle

So what are the main drivers of corporate giving? The Center for Corporate Citizenship at Boston College identified the following drivers for giving:

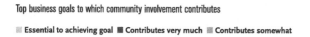

Top business goals to which community involvement contributes

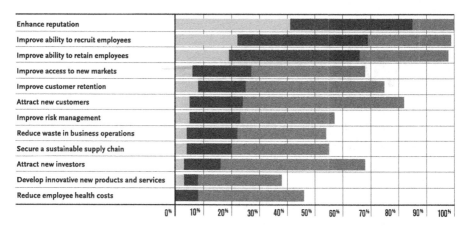

According to Tom Kochan, the George Maverick Bunker Professor of Management at MIT's Sloan School of Management, "If firms do these kinds of things (socially responsible measures) they will get an economic return for their investment and a higher quality workforce that is more loyal and productive. It is a virtuous cycle."[5]

Because of this "virtuous cycle," we believe being a "good corporate citizen" is a concept on the rise in corporate America. There is a community expectation that businesses should play a leadership role in solving our social problems. And, for most companies, it entails cultivating a broad view of the business's self-interest while simultaneously searching for ways to align this self-interest with the larger good.

The Corporate Citizen report (2015) cited above demonstrated that enhancing reputation, improving ability to recruit and retain employees, improving access to new markets, improving customer retention, and attracting new customers, are all viable core reasons for corporations to engage in philanthropy.

A different Boston College report from 2014 indicates that just under 70% of executives view corporate giving as a top priority, sixth on their over-all list of priorities.

The percentage of executives who identify corporate citizenship dimensions as a top priority

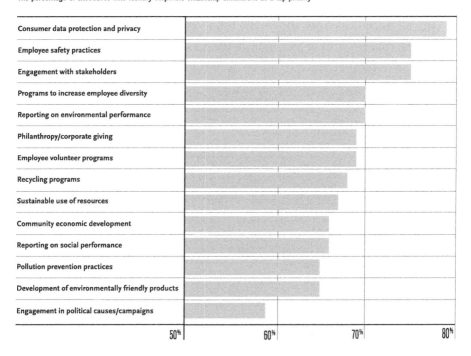

From "The State of Corporate Citizenship 2014." ©2014, Boston College Center for Corporate Citizenship. Reproduced with the permission of Boston College Center for Corporate Citizenship.

The triple bottom line

As these positive leanings toward giving back evolved, John Elkington coined the phrase "triple bottom line: people, planet and profits." The Center for Creative Leadership, in a research white paper entitled "Leadership and the Triple Bottom Line," reports that leaders believe that taking care of profits, people and the planet are critical to organizational success, both now and in the future.[6] Of the hundreds of leaders surveyed:

- 73% tie the triple bottom line to current organizational success

- 87% agree that the concept will be important to organizational success as we move into the future.

This same white paper shows the following list of advantages that businesses will realize from implementing the triple bottom line:

TRIPLE BOTTOM LINE ADVANTAGES	PERCENTAGE
Increased revenue/market share	28%
Increased employee retention	19%
Increased community support	17%
Reduced risk	17%
Other	11%
Positive public relations	6%
Reduced costs	3%
Ease of recruitment	0%
No advantage	0%

Consumers also largely agree that businesses should support the community. According to a 2013 Cone Communications study (see chart on the next page), 94% of consumers want to see more of the businesses they patronize support worthy social and/or environmental issues.[7]

This same study also reports that just 6% of consumers believe businesses exist only to make money, while the clear majority expects companies to do more than just nominally help their communities.

Beliefs about the role of business in society:

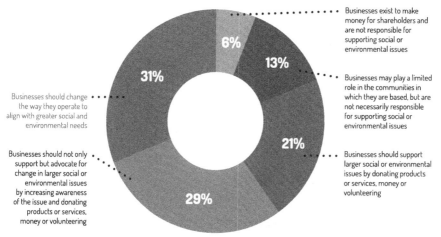

Businesses exist to make money for shareholders and are not responsible for supporting social or environmental issues

Businesses may play a limited role in the communities in which they are based, but are not necessarily responsible for supporting social or environmental issues

Businesses should support larger social or environmental issues by donating products or services, money or volunteering

Businesses should change the way they operate to align with greater social and environmental needs

Businesses should not only support but advocate for change in larger social or environmental issues by increasing awareness of the issue and donating products or services, money or volunteering

6%

13%

31%

21%

29%

From 2013 Cone Communications/Echo Global CSR Study, http://conecomm.com/. Reprinted by permission of Cone Communications.

The "triple bottom line" concept, supported by both businesses and consumers, is also described as being focused on three specific areas:

- Short-term shareholder value

- Social responsibility

- The environment

Sustainability is another popular term for the triple bottom line which includes "going green": being environmentally friendly along with being socially responsible or helping to improve the community. In other words, leaving the planet a better place than before the company began.

There are arguably thousands of books on how to improve shareholder value. The whole field of "going green" or being environmentally sensitive is growing by leaps and bounds with very large businesses such as Walmart and Procter and Gamble, among many others, retooling their businesses to better support the environment. We agree that all three facets of the triple bottom line are important to a healthy society, but because there are many other resources devoted to sustainability, this book will focus on the "socially responsible" portion of the triple bottom line.

There are many, varied reasons why businesses are socially responsible or give back to the community. We group these reasons into three main categories:

1. **Internal Reasons to Give**
    - Improve employee attraction and retention
    - Enhance employee skills

2. **External Reasons to Give**
    - Build brand and corporate image
    - Increase revenue and market share

3. **Moral Reasons to Give**
    - Improve the community
    - Altruism: the right thing to do (and it feels good!)

In the chapters that follow, we'll delve into more detail about each of these categories.

Internal Reasons to Give

2

> "This principle of doing well and doing good holds true for any one person or organization, but it's an especially powerful principle for business and the private sector today. In a business sense, it's the idea that the private sector can be a force for growth and a force for good. That business can make money and make a difference."
>
> - Ajay Banga, CEO of MasterCard

Many companies find that the "people" part of the triple bottom line plays an increasingly crucial role in a business's success as they vie for the right human capital to stay competitive and support their customers with excellence.

Improve employee attraction and retention _____

The Wall Street Journal posited that corporate social responsibility is no longer optional for successful businesses because today's prospective employees, the young generations, are practically requiring that the company they work for stand for something more than just the financial bottom line. In this same article it was reported that more than half of 70 surveyed CEOs said that their employees are the primary motivation for their philanthropy.[8]

A recent *Forbes* study supports this conclusion. It noted that 72% of respondents agreed or strongly agreed, that philanthropy and volunteerism is critical to attracting our newest generations in the workforce, millennials and Gen Y.[9]

The current generation is Generation G, for generosity. "Joining Generation G as a company or a brand is not really optional, it's a fundamental requirement if you want to stay relevant in societies that value generosity, sharing, and collaboration."[10]

In the fifth Millennial Impact Report, more than 50% of the millennial respondents said that a company's involvement in various causes influenced whether or not they accepted a job. By positioning your company as a purposeful corporate citizen, you have a better chance of engaging these potential employees — so much so that millennials are more likely to stick around if they feel like their passions for social good are being fulfilled through your company's mission and everyday operations.

Similarly, in a study conducted by Bentley University, 84% of millennials said that making a positive difference in the world is more important than professional recognition.[11] These statistics make a compelling argument for using philanthropy not only to attract talent, but also to keep it. Millennials aren't going to stay around just for the promise of higher pay or a corner office; rather, they stick around because they see their job as integral to the causes that they support.

By aligning your business to the purpose-driven mindset of this group, and setting up operations in a way that allows employees to see how their work is affecting the world, you set your business up for success in retaining the next generation of talent. Says one millennial in the report, "I took the position here because if a company cares that much about outside causes, I know they are invested in treating me right as an employee."[12]

And yet another organization supports this notion. The Committee Encouraging Corporate Philanthropy (CECP) is a coalition of CEOs who believe that societal improvement is an essential measure of business performance. Michael Stroik, manager of research and analytics for the CECP, reports that millennials are demanding volunteer opportunities as they look for work. He says, "Companies know that they have to build these programs into their workplace if they are to recruit and retain the best talent available."[13]

A Stanford University study reports that current MBA graduates would accept an average of $13,000 less in annual salary to work for a "responsible company."[14]

Not surprisingly, employees agree: a UnitedHealth Group study found that four out of five people who volunteer say they feel better about their employer because of their employer's involvement in volunteer activities.[15]

To be sure, in our discussions with small businesses, we see employee recruitment and retention as *the* primary driver for them to engage in philanthropy. And research supports that approach:

- Sandra Larson Consulting reports that 53% of employees say their loyalty to their employers is strengthened when they are involved in the company's philanthropy.[16]

- Carolyn Cavicchio, in "Building the Business Case for Cause-Related Marketing," reports that:
    - 77% of consumers say a company's support of social issues is a key factor in deciding where to work
    - 80% of consumers would refuse to work at a company which has negative social practices[17]

- A noted researcher on this topic, CONE, finds that 87% of Americans felt that their job loyalty would increase if their company supported activities that improved society.[18]

- Another study found that employees in companies with strong sustainability programs are happier, more satisfied and have higher retention rates.[19]

- The 2014 Millennial Impact Report highlighted the sincerity of philanthropy among millennial workers; most rated an increased desire to be part of greater social change higher than using charitable giving as a way to reduce tax obligations.[20]

Conventional wisdom says that the turnover costs of replacing employees is at least a full year's salary, although CBS News Money Watch estimates the cost to range from 20% of an employee's salary to over 200% for executives.[21] The exact amount depends on how much training the position requires, and how much productivity and knowledge is lost with an employee's departure. In any case, losing even an employee with a $30,000 annual salary would cost at least $6,000. Turnover is very costly to a business in both real costs and lost productivity.

On a practical level, attracting and retaining employees is mission-critical for most companies in today's marketplace. Marian Dozier, Founder and Owner of Austaco, a fast food holding company based in Austin, Texas, believes that philanthropy helps build the spirit of the company. The organization's culture is enhanced by caring about the staff and the community so employees are proud of their employer. Austaco therefore supports not only the community as a whole but also its individual employees. Sure sounds like a triple bottom line company, doesn't it?

The company even goes so far as to provide chaplains to support employees and their families with services such as weddings and funerals — all aimed at helping the staff maintain healthy personal lives. "Giving back gives you goosebumps . . . it makes the hair stand up on your neck," says Marian.

Another company, Zumasys, a cloud-based infrastructure company, agrees. The company allocates one percent of its revenue to philanthropy and 10% of that amount to "people in need in our network" such as relatives, friends, neighbors, and coworkers facing hard times. One Zumasys sales representative found out that one of the company's customers had an employee whose spouse suffered from multiple sclerosis. The employee planned to participate in an MS walk and was searching for sponsors. When CEO Paul Giobbi heard about it from the rep, he not only authorized a company donation, he then made a personal donation as well . . . and accompanied the customer's employee on the walk. After the event, Paul received the following email:

My wife was overwhelmed with emotions when she found out that you traveled all the way from Vegas to join our walk. She had asked if you had a family member or someone you knew personally that was suffering with MS. I simply told her that you do now. I want to personally thank you for taking the time to be with us and acknowledging our cause. The actions you take every day and the generosity you show to your community are a shining example of what we all strive to be as human beings. We are all blessed to have what we have, but to share that with people you don't even know firsthand is truly a miracle at work.[22]

M.P. Mueller, past President of Austin-based advertising agency Door Number 3, concurs that philanthropy helps build the right culture for her company. Job candidates are impressed with Door Number 3's community support, and it makes the company more attractive to work for. Mueller says, "Philanthropy brands you as a company who cares about people, so it's easy to conclude that the company will care about them as employees as well."

She says that giving back serves as a way of employee self-selection — prospective employees who "get it" are drawn to work for Door Number 3 because their values align with the company's vision. Philanthropy is clearly a way to differentiate yourself among employers and attract a more motivated group of employees. "Not only do my employees feel good about working for a company that gives back," says M.P., "but they also work harder for a company that cares."

My (Debbie) personal experience at AT&T and Lucent Technologies confirms the preceding accounts. Our employees really liked our generosity towards the community, which made them want to work for such a company. While we certainly had good pay and good benefits, it was also important to my staff that we were philanthropic.

According to CECP's Michael Stroik, "A highly engaged workforce is more likely to exert extra effort and have lower turnover rates, which can be linked to increased output, sales, and profitability."[23]

Cardinal Health, a healthcare support company headquartered in Columbus, Ohio has detected higher company loyalty and employee satisfaction scores as a result of their intentional commitment to strategic philanthropy.

Another Austin firm, ABC Home & Commercial Services, a provider of pest control and other home support services, agrees that the staff feels good about the company, which tends to "lock the employees into the business," says company President Bobby Jenkins.

Enhance employee skills

There are all kinds of ways to get your employees trained: formal company-led training programs (think McDonald's University), on-the-job learning, experiential programs, job swaps, attending conferences, or reading relevant materials.

Another very effective way to learn new skills is by participating outside the business in philanthropy. This role could be anything from front-line, hands-on volunteering; participating in a team event sorting food; board service; or anything in between.

Each type of service leads to developing different skill sets. I (Debbie) have helped build many Habitat for Humanity homes, volunteered in food pantries, and served food to the homeless (in addition to going on several mission trips). This hands-on volunteering has taught me patience, understanding, how to be a good team player, and communication skills, as well as the particular physical skills we were using such as hammering, roofing, etc. I have also been honored to serve on more than a dozen boards of directors of nonprofits. This board service, because it is governance-oriented, has taught me leadership skills such as building consensus, negotiating, re-solving conflict, financial management, leading meetings, etc. All of these skills have served me well over the years, not only professionally but per-sonally as well.

An interesting study by Pillsbury of its employee volunteers found that 91% reported that volunteering enabled them to develop their skillsets in:

- management

- teamwork

- problem-solving

- strategic action[24]

Another 2010 study reports that employees especially value volunteer-ing that provides skill development, networking opportunities and social interaction.[25]

The *Forbes* document mentioned previously indicates a strong belief that employee skill development is one business goal that may be reached through philanthropy. Fifty-nine percent (59%) of businesses reported that increasing employee skill development and leadership is a goal of their philanthropy.[26]

From the company's viewpoint, 89% of supervisors say that employee volunteers engage in positive work behaviors more often than employees who do not volunteer.[27]

More positive impact from volunteering is also demonstrated by:

- A study of young people's volunteering reported that between 79% and 91% of the respondents believed their confidence, com-munication skills, and ability to work with others had improved as a result of their charity work.[28]

- Deloitte Points of Light Foundation says 63% of its respondents reported that volunteering has had a positive impact on their careers.[29]

- A UnitedHealth Group study found that 87% of people who volunteered in the last year said that their volunteering has helped develop their teamwork and people skills.[30]

It was my (Debbie) personal experience that philanthropic volunteering greatly enhanced my employees' skills. On one occasion, I had a manager who wanted to improve her speaking skills and broaden her management perspective. We decided that becoming a "loaned executive" during the United Way's annual campaign would likely be a good fit for this goal and we figured out a way to give her up for many months to make this happen. She returned to work energized and very grateful for the experience and, more importantly, her role on the campaign improved not only the skills she sought but many others that served her well back on her regular job with AT&T.

Companies win by getting more skilled employees, and employees themselves win by becoming increasingly skilled at their work and in their contributions.

Improve employee outlook _____

Beyond simply improving our skills, Dr. Christine Carter with the Greater Good Science Center reports that doing something nice for someone else actually benefits our health. Volunteers report feeling a "helpers' high," including feeling stronger, more energetic, calmer, less depressed, and even an increased sense of self-worth. Part of her study showed that seniors (55 and older) who volunteered for two or more organizations reduced their chance of dying by an impressive 44% — almost as beneficial as quitting smoking, a traditional life extender.[31]

Along the same lines, the Future World Giving website reports that clinical studies show making a donation to charity causes pleasure centers in the brain to light up. And another study found that people who were given money and asked to make a donation with it reported feeling much happier than those who were asked to keep the same sum of money for themselves.[32]

Increase productivity

Another big win for businesses is increased employee productivity. In a recent study covered by The Conversation, employees performed better in terms of production output if they had charitable donations as part of their compensation package.[33]

Similarly, a study by the University of Southampton also reinforces the idea that when workers are given a social incentive such as a charitable donation linked to their job, performance increases by an average of 13% — and up to 30% among those who were initially the least productive. Performance was most improved (by 26%) when workers were allowed to decide for themselves how much of their pay they wanted to contribute.[34]

According to Charities Aid Foundation, "The argument follows thusly: when people give time and money to charity or engage in philanthropy it makes them happier, better connected, healthier, and more resilient. This, in turn, makes them more productive and less likely to rely on the welfare state. No brainer."[35]

> Truepoint Capital, a wealth management company from Cincinnati, Ohio, so strongly believes that nonprofit involvement leads to professional development that over 50% of its employees are engaged in some kind of philanthropic service.

One of Austin's premier business philanthropists, ABC Home & Commercial Services, supports employee groups volunteering because the President, Bobby Jenkins, strongly believes that working together for community good strengthens teamwork far beyond on-the-job opportunities. He says that no matter how hard or exhausting the task, his teams come back into the workplace with renewed enthusiasm and better teamwork.

For example, ABC regularly takes work groups to Caritas of Austin to help prepare and serve lunch to members of Austin's homeless population. Bobby has no doubt that the shared experience of doing good together solidifies team relationships — and, in turn, brings these benefits back to the business. "As a business owner, I strongly support having my employees

volunteer together," says Bobby. "They invariably come back to work energized, working more closely and productively as a team, and feeling good
about working for ABC because we support the community."

Another Austin firm, Gammon Insurance, a Higginbotham Company,
uses the Junior League to support the development of female employees.
The Junior League is well known for its leadership development of women
so Billy Gammon, the company's Founder, encourages his female employees to participate in the Junior League, supporting both the community
through the good work of the Junior League's initiatives and his own employees through further skill development.

Showing significant commitment, MARS, a marketing agency based in
Southfield, Michigan, gives employees the opportunity to take a month-long
sabbatical at the charitable organization of their choice. Account Manager
Kasia Koziatek says the experiences have boosted morale, fostered team-
work, and improved camaraderie. "It's created a tighter organization," says
MARS CEO Rob Rivenburgh.[36]

Khadija Al Arkoubi, Assistant Professor of Management at the University of New Haven, reinforces this point: "Allowing it (volunteering) improves
their employees' engagement and well-being. They also develop their soft
skills, including their leadership capabilities."[37]

Key points _____

- Research suggests that businesses can better attract and retain employees because of their philanthropy.

- Employees will enhance their skills by participating in philanthropy.

- Employees will also improve their mental outlook and productivity.

External Reasons to Give

3

"This is the true joy in life, being used for a purpose recognized by yourself as a mighty one; being thoroughly worn out before you are thrown on the scrap heap; being a force of Nature instead of a feverish selfish little clod of ailments and grievances complaining that the world will not devote itself to making you happy."

- George Bernard Shaw, author and playwright

While there are benefits to giving that improve the employees themselves and the appeal of your company to them, of course, programs that enhance a business's ability to make money (external reasons to give) are going to be a priority. Philanthropy programs not only enhance the company's brand and image but also increase market share and revenues.

Build brand and corporate image

Corporate citizenship, especially today, is noticeably central to a company's reputation. In our current highly interconnected world, reputation is at once more valuable and more vulnerable to losing quickly over the slightest misstep which can be shared around the globe within seconds. Almost three-quarters of CEOs (74%) participate in corporate social responsibility (CSR) because they believe it drives company reputation and image.[38]

The latest study by the Boston College Center for Corporate Citizenship finds that over 80% of businesses support corporate citizenship because it 'enhances reputation' (only slightly behind the first reason, attracting new customers, at 85%). While priorities have shifted slightly over the years, corporate reputation has consistently been a key driver of corporate citizenship since the 2009 study.

Importance of business goals

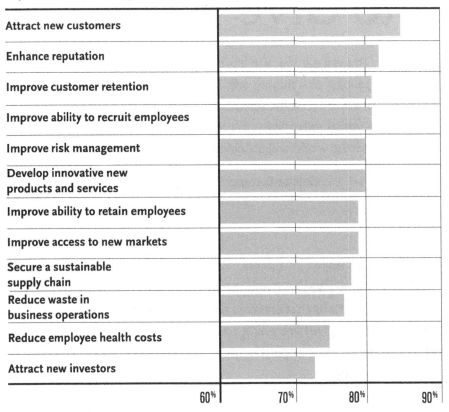

From "The State of Corporate Citizenship 2014." ©2014, Boston College Center for Corporate Citizenship. Reproduced with the permission of Boston College Center for Corporate Citizenship.

Along these same lines, Matteo Tonello, Research Director of Corporate Leadership at The Conference Board, says, "A coherent corporate contribution program is a formidable way for a corporation to enhance its business strategy and reward loyal stakeholders."[39]

The aforementioned *Forbes* report reinforces the linkage between corporate philanthropy and company brand, noting the highest two responses from the top level management surveyed about how philanthropy enhances reputation and brand is through corporate citizenship and social responsibility.[40]

As further emphasis of the point, *USA Today* columnist Gladys Edmunds suggested that one of four principle strategies for a company to remain visible in today's society is to "support a charity."[41]

As mentioned earlier, 93% of consumers expect businesses to support the community.[7]

Stephen Graves, author of *The Business of Generosity*, also reinforces this point when he reports that a friend told him, "Our cause alignment and giving is part of our personal brand . . . Someone might say I support charity: water or I care about human trafficking. If you get that, then you get me better."[42]

Not surprisingly, there are many examples of companies who believe that giving back will enhance their brand and reputation. Air Comfort, a heating and air conditioning company in St. Louis, Missouri, created a branding program with Honor Flight, an organization that flies veterans to Washington D.C. to see the memorials that honor them. Both organizations partnered with Incite, a cause marketing firm that uses advertising for good. Incite helped design a campaign which was all about branding Honor Flight and Air Comfort together and informing consumers that purchases made during a designated time period would fund Honor flights for area veterans. Corey Malone, President of Air Comfort, says, "I would much rather invest my time and effort, and my company's time and effort, into an organization that pays back." This association with a popular cause creates a positive buzz for their brand in the community, lifting sales all while helping veterans.

Also, to this end, many companies use natural synergies between their product or service and their philanthropy to enhance their brand: Eastside Lumber donates lumber to Habitat for Humanity. Toys R Us works with Toys for Tots at Christmastime. 9Lives cat food supports cat shelters. Philadel-phia Cream Cheese partners with nonprofits trying to end child hunger.

Milk + Honey, a salon/spa located in Austin, Texas is another good example of this attention to brand. At its inception, the business found itself reacting to a constant stream of solicitations for donations. It was able to support many of these requests by offering non-cash, donated spa or salon services which enhanced its brand and reputation as the donations were fulfilled. As the company matured, however, Co-Founder and Owner Alissa Bayer realized that its efforts were spread so far and wide that they lacked any particular impact. So she transitioned toward supporting a few, strategically chosen nonprofits. Not only do they appreciate the impact, but the "win-win is finding opportunities for visibility," says Bayer. This new, more focused giving strategy further enhances Milk + Honey's brand in more impactful ways.

Also cognizant of the importance of philanthropy's contribution to its brand, Creative Suitcase, an Austin-based graphic design agency, chooses only one nonprofit to receive a substantial donation each year, in the name of its current clients. It then uses the opportunity to publicize its choice to clients, partners and friends via a holiday marketing piece designed by staff.

For example, over the years, they have created an on-line story, a holiday ornament, a puzzle, and a greeting card. The year of the greeting card, designed for Austin Pets Alive, Creative Suitcase took it a step further and also sold the cards as a fundraiser for the organization.

President Rachel Clemens says, "The holiday projects are always a resounding success. It allows us to do what we do best: be creative! Our clients and friends have come to expect them." And as proof that philanthropy can build a company's brand, Creative Suitcase's projects have won several advertising industry awards.

Rachel continues, "Our goal is to showcase our capabilities in a really fun, engaging way while hopefully raising some awareness for our chosen nonprofit as well. Think about doing what employees and clients love so it will be a home run for everyone."

You can see how the work builds their brand, all while doing good.

Competitive differentiation

Part of good branding is competitive differentiation. A widely known success story that built its brand on philanthropy is TOM's Shoes, which gives
away one pair of footwear to the indigent for every pair sold. As its "one for
one" giving model has grown in popularity (think Warby Parker and others),
research shows that 80% of U.S. adults would favor a brand associated with
a good cause over another one of similar price and quality. Nineteen percent said they would switch to a more expensive brand to support a cause.[43]

And a different study, Nielsen's 2012 Global Consumer survey, showed
that 66% of worldwide consumers prefer to buy products and services from
companies that give back to society.[44]

In my (Debbie) experience across several different cities with AT&T and
then Lucent Technologies, customers were routinely willing to pay more for
our product and service — anywhere from 10-15% more than our competi-

tors. This was partly due to our market leader position and our strength of offerings, but it is my opinion that it was also due to our visibility in the community and the fact that we were generous in helping all citizens live better lives.

An even more recent study conducted by CONE Communications in 2015, found that 90% of Americans were likely to switch brands to one associated with a cause if the price and quality were the same (even though this percentage is slightly reduced from previous years).

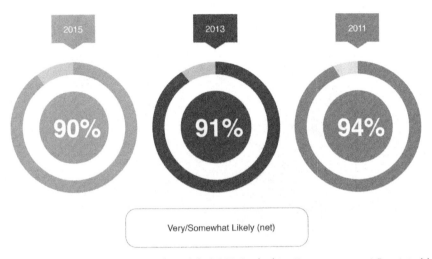

From 2015 Cone Communications/Echo Global CSR Study, http://conecomm.com/. Reprinted by permission of Cone Communications.

The previously mentioned *Forbes* report indicates a strong correlation, with 78% of respondents agreeing or strongly agreeing that community and philanthropic efforts are critical to the way their company differentiates itself in the marketplace.[45]

Consumers on another study indicate a strong preference for "do-gooder" businesses as a differentiator. A specific study done for Hershey's Company found that once consumers were aware of its philanthropy, their purchase intent and brand loyalty showed significant increases.[46]

In fact, all of these factors lead to additional customers and attracting new customers is the top business goal for corporate philanthropy according to the most recent State of Corporate Citizenship graph referenced earlier in this chapter on page 26.

Other external benefits

Businesses can also capitalize on other external benefits of charitable giving, including the creation of community support, the ability to mitigate bad publicity, and the ability to increase revenue and market share.

1. **Create community support.** It would seem that the government is more amenable to supporting the business needs of companies that support the community. Both AMD and Samsung leveraged their strong community support of Austin, Texas as they were able to successfully get new buildings approved through what is often a contentious planning process.

   Anecdotally, AT&T has long been a strong supporter of the community with large philanthropic donations. I (Debbie) worked for AT&T for many years and was so proud to work for a company that supported the community in such visible and meaningful ways. Back in the late 2000's, AT&T wanted to be a leader in the public policy discussions about the "information superhighway." Through having CEO Bob Allen volunteer to work on the well-being of children with the Clinton-Gore administration, he was then invited to be at the table when the decision was made to make the information superhighway a private rather than public initiative. AT&T was very sincere in its support of the community while also building corporate influence toward business-affecting issues.

2. **Mitigate bad publicity.** Many companies today seek to restore a tarnished image by promoting how they "do good" in the community. Stanford Graduate School of Business Professor Ed deHaan's recent study found that fence-mending efforts from large public corporations aimed at the community (including employees and customers) were very important to rebuilding their reputation.

   But surprisingly, companies see even more encouraging results when their philanthropy is in response to scandal than when it comes from genuine altruism. Positive returns in this circumstance, on average, were a two percent increase in share prices, indicating enhanced investor confidence.[47]

According to one CONE Communications study, 42% of consumers say they have boycotted a company's products or services in the past year after learning it had behaved in a way deemed irresponsible.[48] A more recent CONE survey looks at the issue of consumer reaction to bad behavior from both sides per the following chart:

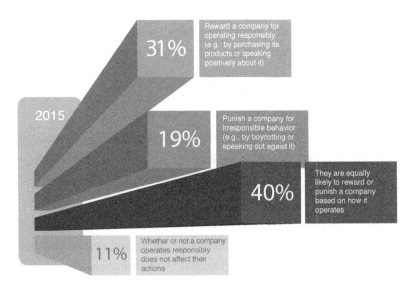

Consumers will reward or punish based on companies' CSR efforts and operations.

2015

31% Reward a company for operating responsibly (e.g., by purchasing its products or speaking positively about it)

19% Punish a company for irresponsible behavior (e.g., by boycotting or speaking out against it)

40% They are equally likely to reward or punish a company based on how it operates

11% Whether or not a company operates responsibly does not affect their actions

From 2015 Cone Communications / Echo Global CSR Study, http://conecomm.com/. Reprinted by permission of Cone Communications.

All in all, brand, reputation, image and competitive advantage are inextricably intertwined.

Truepoint Capital, of Cincinnati, Ohio, ensures that its philanthropy is consistent with its mission because the synergies deepen the client relationship.

Cardinal Health of Columbus, Ohio, says that its reputation is positively affected by philanthropy, even if this was not the motivation behind it.

Best Upon Request, a business concierge provider headquartered in Cincinnati, Ohio, also says the side benefit of philanthropy is positive company branding, though this was not the impetus for giving back either.

Door Number 3 puts an interesting twist on highlighting its generosity to clients. After "adopting" 30 underprivileged kids for the holidays, the company used the kids' photos in holiday cards to clients, both thanking the clients for making it all possible while letting them know about Door Number 3's generosity.

ABC Home & Commercial Services supported the Tour de Cure bike ride, benefitting the American Diabetes Association. Employees both participated as riders in the race and also staffed the water stops. This visibility throughout all facets of the race helped build the company brand while also promoting employee bonding.

Increase revenue and market share _____

While the research needed to directly tie philanthropy to increased financials is difficult to structure and execute, there have been a few studies
undertaken to gather this data. In 2010, Accenture Sustainability Services
compared the business performance of a representative cross-section of
275 companies from the Fortune Global 1000. The study, "Can Business Do
Well By Doing Good?" found that the 50 companies which ranked highest in
sustainability leadership outperformed their peers in shareholder returns.
The top 50 sustainability companies' three-year shareholder returns exceeded the bottom 50 companies by 16 percentage points and exceeded
the middle 50 firms by six percentage points.[49]

Similarly, the recent CECP study showed incrementally better revenue
and profit results for those companies that were most philanthropic:

The Most Generous Companies in 2010 Realized Strong Business Returns from 2010 to 2013

	Change in Revenues from 2010 to 2013	Change in Pre-Tax Profits from 2010 to 2013
2010 Most Generous Companies (75th Percentile)	+3%	+4%
2010 Least Generous Companies (25th Percentile)	-3%	+1%

*From Emerging Trends in Corporate Contributions, CECP, https://www.michiganfoundations.org. Re-
printed by permission of CECP.*

Baruch Lev, Phillip Bardes Professor of Accounting and Finance at the
New York University Stern School of Business puts it this way: "The evidence shows that, done the right way, corporate contributions can indeed
be good for both the company performance and society." He has also con-
cluded research in conjunction with The University of Texas at Dallas that
showed a positive correlation between a company's charitable giving budget and future sales.[50]

Clearly, companies also believe that giving back produces tangible returns. The previously mentioned *Forbes* study of 2011 substantiates this statement, finding that 93% of companies believe they can "create economic value by creating societal value."[51]

And the recent study from Boston College, noted earlier, also reinforces this belief about possible tangible and intangible contributions of corporate goodwill to reputation and the business' bottom line:

Market value of top global brands
Intangible and tangible value ($bn)

■ **Intangible value**   ▨ **Tangible value**

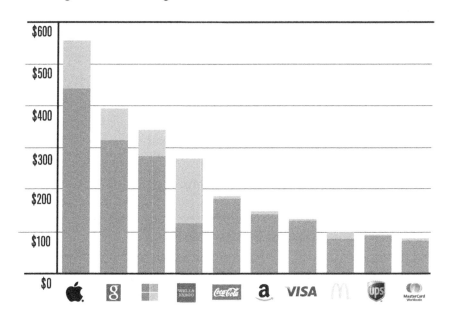

Chart note: Brands are among the top 20 of BrandZ's *Top 100 Most Valuable Global Brands 2014*. Retrieved from Millward Brown website, https://www.millwardbrown.com/brandz/2014/Top100/Docs/2014_BrandZ_Top100_Chart.pdf

Source (for market market value of companies on June 30, 2014): Retrieved from ycharts.com

Source (for equity, net intangibles, and goodwill for tangible/intangible value calculations, 2nd quarter 2014 balance sheets [end of June 2014]): *Symbol lookup* (n.d.). Retrieved from http://www.nasdaq.com/symbol/

"Being socially responsible is both a moral and business imperative. Any company that doesn't strive to be a good corporate citizen risks undermining its reputation and jeopardizing its profitability over the long run," says Jay Hooley, Chairman and CEO of State Street Corporation.[52]

The Jim Butler Auto Group of St. Louis, Missouri was able to measure increased revenue through philanthropy. They partnered with Incite, mentioned earlier, to develop and promote a teen safe driving program, especially encouraging teens to avoid calling, texting, tweeting or posting while driving. The high school with the most signed pledges received a $10,000 scholarship. The campaign resulted in 75,000 signed pledges and an 11% increase in sales. Because of its success they will be continuing into the second year and plan to expand it regionally to other dealerships.

Door Number 3's M.P. Mueller noted that while increased revenue is not the driver behind their philanthropy, occasionally new business does result. As an example, the firm donated a marketing campaign to the Austin Humane Society. Not only was that work useful in obtaining future business because she could tell pet-loving decision makers immediately had an emotional connection to the firm, but in fact the Austin Humane Society hired Door Number 3 for additional paid work. So you can see how increased revenue may happen, whether specifically intended or not.

There is no question in Bobby Jenkins' mind, President of ABC Home & Commercial Services, that "consumers will choose to do business with those who support the community."

Standard Heating, a heating, ventilation and air conditioning provider in Minneapolis, Minnesota also feels strongly that giving back should be synergistic with the company mission. According to Vice President Todd Ferrara, "It's partly about making a buck, but also about making a difference."

A relevant quote comes from Dick Rathgeber, a notable Austin philan-thropist, who has been know to quip, "Cast your bread upon the waters and it will come back as chocolate cake."

Another quote from the former CEO of Walmart, Mike Duke, also sup-ports this point: "Being involved in social issues isn't counter to being prof-itable; it actually causes Walmart to be a better business. We strive to run a better business, to be more profitable, and to serve customers better."[53] Once again, the triple bottom line appears to be supported by Walmart.

And one last quote on the subject, MARS CEO Rob Rivenburgh says, "Our program helps us recruit the best of class. Every company should have a formalized social responsibility program; the return on investment is pro-found."[54]

Key points

- Companies enhance their reputation and image by being viewed as good corporate citizens.

- Studies show a correlation between giving back and increased rev-enue.

Moral reasons to give

4

> "The practice of charity will bind us . . . will bind all men in one great brotherhood."
>
> - Conrad Hilton, hotelier

While improving the company's resources, both people (employee skill improvement and attraction) and profit (enhanced company reputation and revenue), are important, there are many firms who believe that giving back is a moral imperative. One aspect of this obligation is that helping the community be a better place to work and live for all residents also helps create better consumers to buy their products and/or services. But many leaders also believe that if they have been blessed enough to have good resources at their disposal, they are morally obligated to utilize those resources to the betterment of society. The adage "as you give, so shall you receive" comes to mind.

The fact that consumers expect businesses to give back in support of the community further reinforces the moral imperative.

Improve the community

Andrew Carnegie, arguably one of our country's great philanthropists, stated that the rich who had prospered through their talents in business should use those same talents to help others improve their own lives. He also felt that they should dispose of their surplus wealth by giving it away during their lifetimes. This philosophy has become popular again with current corporate leaders, including Bill Gates, who is making huge investments in education and healthcare in order to see results while he is still living.

Interestingly, a recent Boston College report notes that global consumers largely believe businesses have a major role to play in solving societal issues, even if company leaders don't agree at the same level. As our world continues to become even more consumer-driven, we might expect business leadership to change their outlook.

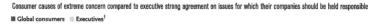

Consumer causes of extreme concern compared to executive strong agreement on issues for which their companies should be held responsible
■ Global consumers ■ Executives†

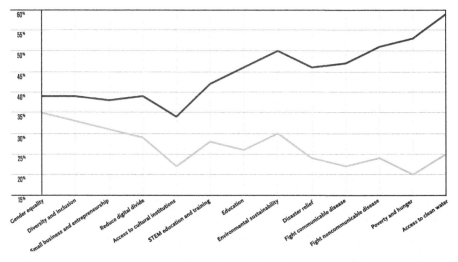

From "The State of Corporate Citizenship 2014." ©2014, Boston College Center for Corporate Citizenship. Reproduced with the permission of Boston College Center for Corporate Citizenship

It is intuitive that having a better community with citizens who are thriving will make for better customers and a better place to work and live. Certainly the CEO of Starbucks, Howard Schultz, agrees: "It is no longer enough to serve customers, employees, and shareholders. As corporate citizens of the world, it is our responsibility — our duty — to serve the communities where we do business by helping to improve, for example, the quality of citizens' education, employment, health care, safety, and overall daily life, plus future prospects."[55]

In the following chart, from a more recent Boston College report, we can see in which issues businesses think they should be involved:

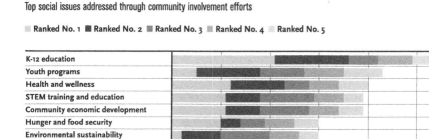

Top social issues addressed through community involvement efforts

Ranked No. 1   Ranked No. 2   Ranked No. 3   Ranked No. 4   Ranked No. 5

From "The Corporate Citizen" ©2015, Boston College Center for Corporate Citizenship, 2015. Reproduced with the permission of Boston College Center for Corporate Citizenship.

According to an earlier report from Boston College, public opinion polling data clearly indicates that expectations will continue to rise for companies to do more to address economic and social challenges, both domestically and globally.[56]

Individual companies clearly agree that doing good for the community is appropriate. Buffie Blesi, President of Knowledge Sphere, a Minneapolis-based business coaching firm, got the "bug" to give when she was in college working in the financial aid office and noting how much her work meant to those she helped obtain financing. She saw firsthand how critical a loan could be to helping the applicants get their advanced education. She vowed then that if she was financially successful in her career, she would help others finance their university-level learning. She has since brought this concept forward into her business and fulfilled the commitment she made of helping improve the community by giving others the advantage of a college education.

Two exemplary companies in particular who have formulated their entire business plan around the community are Give Something Back and Keeper Springs. Give Something Back, an office supply company headquartered in Sacramento, California uses its business capacity to make money and then gives 100% of its profits to nonprofits who know best how to support the community's needs. Keeper Springs, a bottled water provider based in Boston, Massachusetts also gives away 100% of its profits to help the community by protecting our waterways, focusing on environmental issues including recycling and conservation.

As a healthcare company, Cardinal Health naturally chose two very specific ways to help the community: 1) increase efficiency and effectiveness within hospitals; and 2) reduce prescription drug abuse. Both of these goals clearly are all about improving the community.

Jancoa, a janitorial company in Cincinnati, Ohio, is similar to UMoveItWeCleanIt (see below) in providing opportunities for jobs to those who are having a tough time staying employed. CEO Mary Miller and her husband train their staff well and believe in the concept of "teaching a man to fish." They are so gratified to see peoples' lives changing for the better as they watch their associates buy their first home or go to college for the first time in their family. According to Miller, "Positive energy comes from doing better in life, which in turn creates an upward spiral, fueling better things to happen over and over."

And another shining example is UMoveItWeCleanIt in Austin, Texas. CEO Sheri Marshall believes that everyone deserves a second chance, so she offers training and job opportunities mainly for women and men who are getting out of jail after being incarcerated. She and her husband train workers on cleaning methods and chemicals but — probably more importantly — also on expectations for getting and holding a job, attributes such as honesty, dependability, courtesy, communication, and other important characteristics. In this way, her firm is improving the community by helping a hard-to-employ segment of the population find jobs. Sheri says, "My mission is helping people in distress to be free of that distress, which benefits the public good."

This quote from Bobby Jenkins, President of ABC Home & Commercial Services, shows that he agrees: "Our business thrives because of the wonderful community that is Austin, and I can't think of anything more gratifying than being able to give back to the community so that it's a great place to live for everyone."

Altruism: it is the right thing to do

John F. Kennedy said, paraphrasing the Bible, "To whom much is given, much is expected." The Bible passage referenced is Luke 12:48, which says "To whoever much is given, of him will much be required; and to whom much was entrusted, of him more will be asked" (World English Bible).[57]

This notion of giving back is seen throughout all different belief systems, so it should not be surprising that many Americans believe that successful businesses should give back to the communities that help them thrive.

Philanthropy, after all, means "love of mankind." So a belief system grounded in loving one another might logically make one feel obligated to help our fellow man.

Tim Shriver, son of Sargent Shriver, a former U.S. ambassador to France, credits Catholicism for his family's commitment. He says, "What our Catholic tradition has done well is make you not just *ought* to help, but *want* to help — hunger for it. Be hungry for justice, be hungry for healing, be hungry for connection, be hungry for leveling the playing field. That's more than just a moral imperative. It's believing that your best self will always be in solidarity with those who are having a hard time. After all, Jesus was all about [taking care of] the poor and the marginalized and then having a party."[58]

Statistical studies back up that most people expect such altruism:

- 80% of consumers say larger companies should do more than give money to solve social problems, advocating for donating talent, volunteers and the like.

- 89% of Americans say it is important for businesses, government and nonprofits to collaborate to solve our social and environmental issues.

- 79% of business leaders say the public should expect good citizenship from companies.[59]

Just like we, as individuals, are inclined to give because we know it is the right thing to do, it appears that we ascribe this same concept to business entities as well.

Michael Porter and Mark Kramer write in the *Harvard Business Review*, "When a well-run business applies its vast resources, expertise, and management talent to problems that it understands and in which it has a stake, it can have a greater impact on social good than any other institution or philanthropic organization."[60]

And in practice, contemporary philanthropists Pierre Omidyar and Jeff Skoll, Co-Founders of eBay, believe that philanthropy can affect social good through for-profit activities as well as through monetary giving. The Austin, Texas office provides a great example of this philosophy. In 2013, it implemented a "Small Business Challenge." It allowed employees to team up in groups of five and donate their skills to six elected nonprofits. These teams dedicated 10% of their work time over a six month period to discover the challenges of their chosen nonprofit, design technology solutions to help, and deliver the work-product to overcome these challenges.

In addition, the Austin eBay office matches all employee donations of up to $2,500 per year; awards grants from its own foundation (totaling

$40,000) to select Austin nonprofits based on employee nominations and voting; and has a philanthropy committee that plans three to four charity projects each quarter — such as Coats for Kids, toy drives, fundraisers and more — to benefit the nonprofit community.

Sharon Watkins, Owner of the iconic Chez Zee restaurant in Austin, Texas, says she's a "do-gooder at heart," so it was natural for her to incorporate philanthropy into her business.

Glenn Garland, CEO of CLEAResult, an energy company also in Austin, says he feels "we should be good stewards and give back because it's the right thing to do." He adds that altruism is the driver of the company's giving, *not* publicity.

Jeff Hahn, Principal of Hahn Texas, an Austin-based public relations firm, comes at philanthropy from a similar — though slightly different — angle. His viewpoint is that being blessed with the talents, skills, and means to give back creates an obligation to contribute to the societal good.

Tillie Hidalgo Lima, President and CEO of Best Upon Request, of Cincinnati, Ohio, learned to give back from her parents. They immigrated from Cuba and found a wonderful new life in America. Grateful to their new country and circumstances, they felt strongly that it was incumbent upon them to give back to help others who had not had all their advantages. This altruism was ingrained in their children as well. So when Tillie became the leader of her firm, she weaved philanthropy into the fabric of her business.

Her giving includes monetary donations through a robust employee giving campaign in conjunction with the United Way, personal leadership donations to a number of nonprofits, and volunteering, both via many of her staff who volunteer as well as her own service on several nonprofit boards and leading initiatives such as co-chairing the YWCA Women of Achievement awards and the St. Ursula school capital campaign. Tillie says "It's part of my heart and I feel called to serve as a leader in order to make a difference and leave the world a better place." A side benefit for her is that she is surrounded by generous people which she enjoys as a result of this philosophy that drives the company culture.

P.D. Morrison runs an office supply company in Austin, Texas and learned to give back at the feet of his grandfather, who helped people in need from the grocery store he owned. P.D. used to observe baskets of food being assembled at the grocery store and assumed they would be for sale. What he discovered was that they were being donated to families who needed a little extra help just then. So this obligation to give back was ingrained early and permeates not only his business giving but also his personal life.

On the business front, his firm has a robust philanthropy program, including donations to research certain diseases that have touched his family (leukemia, diabetes, and macular degeneration), support for a Habitat for Humanity house build, mentoring other businesses and individuals, and donating school supplies to a number of children-oriented nonprofits. On the personal side, P.D. has taken his altruism to the nth degree by even adopting hard-to-place foster children versus having his own biological children in support of the community good.

Our personal observation is that altruistic support of the community tends to spring from one of two foundations:

1. Family members who exemplify and model compassionate giving; or

2. Religious encouragement to help others less fortunate.

I (Debbie) will freely admit that I was raised with the belief that if I was blessed enough to be successful, I was expected to give back. Whatever the reason for your philanthropy, your motivations will help inform the rest of your philanthropy planning process. And, as Tom Kochan of MIT said, "It (corporate social responsibility) is a virtuous cycle." After all, the whole community benefits from our businesses' generosity.[5]

Key points

- Many firms believe that by helping to improve the community, they help themselves, too: a healthier community buys more and is a better place for their employees to live.

- Many givers believe that giving back is simply the right thing to do — they have been blessed and feel obligated to share their good fortune.

G is for Gear-Up

5

> "If you think of life as like a big pie, you can try to hold the whole pie and kill yourself trying to keep it, or you can slice it up and give some to the people around you, and you still have plenty left for yourself."

- Jay Leno, comedian

We have reviewed the benefits of giving back: internally improving employee skills and their attraction to your company, externally enhancing your reputation and revenue, and addressing a moral imperative to improve the community to help make it a better place in which to live and work.

So what's next? According to the "Director Notes" report from The Conference Board, "Given the evolving expectations for corporate philanthropy, corporate giving programs must go beyond simply doing good." The further exhortation is that, in order to ensure the effectiveness of corporate philanthropy programs, executives should apply the same prudence to giving decisions that they do to other business activities.[61]

Doing good can be accomplished, one might contend, by just writing checks to nonprofits when solicited. But in order to really be effective, you must first develop a strategic philanthropy plan. Just as you would not run your company without a strategy, why would you invest your hard earned money and other precious resources in the community without a strategy?

Rachel Clemens, President of Creative Suitcase, says, "You need to treat philanthropy just like any other business priority: commit, plan and execute."

Sharon Watkins of Chez Zee restaurant reinforces the same concept: "You should match your philanthropy to the business and do what makes sense, creating a strategic plan to identify what you want from your giving and making sure you get it."

UMoveItWeCleanIt CEO Sheri Marshall advises thinking of corporate giving as a process rather than a one-time shot. With a never-ending need for community support, philanthropy should be an iterative cycle.

P.D. Morrison of P.D. Morrison Enterprises, Inc. notes that "the more you can develop philanthropy programs based on the company's core competencies, the more sustainable they become." This synergy enables a business to stick with giving even in tough times.

Gammon Insurance also supports the long-term nature of giving back. "Do it consistently over time so you become known for it," says CEO Billy Gammon. Clients still thank him today for sponsoring their Little League baseball teams when they were children — witness to the longevity of his philanthropy.

In fact, the book *The Business of Generosity* notes one of three main trends occurring in business philanthropy is the shift from *indiscriminate* giving to *strategic* giving.[62]

The Conference Board, mentioned above, says "A well-designed program clearly articulates congruence between the company's philanthropic activities and its other business activities," reinforcing the point that some forethought is needed.[63]

In order to give your philanthropy thorough deliberation, we recommend that you follow the GIVES model in developing your philanthropy strategy:

The first step in developing a philanthropy strategy is the "G" in our GIVES model: Gear-up. This phase is all about getting started on the right foot by determining what causes grab your attention and really light your fire.

Gear-Up Step 1: Who do you currently give to? ____

The first step in the process of gearing-up is to identify to whom you already give. The exercise naturally entails some introspection because looking at who you have been giving to will elicit both positive and negative emotions associated with those gifts. Even when it's uncomfortable, though, the past should inform and influence your future giving.

Our own business has decided on a philosophy of donating to organizations that share our desire for improved philanthropy and more resources to the Austin community. So each year we have given to several organizations that are committed to helping both businesses and individuals more easily give back in support of our society. An example of this is Little Helping Hands, which provides volunteer opportunities for families with small children and, through its work, is helping shape the next generation of philanthropists. This methodology is synergistic with our own business vision and works well for us because otherwise, between the two principals, we would have too many worthy causes we would love to support to do so effectively.

As you review your current philanthropic investments, you will find that some have made a significant impact and are easy to support again, while others may have left a sense of dissatisfaction. Each business has a slightly different idea about what makes for a successful connection and a desire for an on-going relationship.

Personal connection. Bulldog Solutions, a marketing firm in Austin, Texas has found a cause that really engages its employees. One of the founder's friends has a daughter who was diagnosed with Batten's disease. This often fatal ailment is a nervous system disorder that causes seizures and eventual loss of motor skills. Company employees wanted to fund research toward a cure, so they created "Run to the Sun," an overnight relay run from Mt. Bonnell in the heart of Austin to Enchanted Rock in the heart of the Texas Hill Country.

This 100-mile run gave employees plenty of time to bond while running together in the middle of the night. Its uniqueness (running through the night) also made it popular and exciting. Bulldog Solutions found that beyond the funds raised, the positive buzz that came back into the office and continued for many months afterward made it both worthwhile as a cause to support and extremely feasible to repeat.

Synergistic goals. BuildASign, a signage maker in Austin, Texas has also developed a great fit for its philanthropy. While it supports many nonprofits, one in particular has become a regular recipient of BuildA-Sign's giving. And interestingly, the nonprofit found BuildASign rather than the reverse.

The Leukemia/Lymphoma Society reached out to BuildASign a number of years ago to request donated signage for one of their big annual walks called "Light the Night." BuildASign's policy is not to donate products totally free, but instead to offer a substantial (40-50%) discount for the signage. Both organizations took the time to really get to know one another's culture and, therefore, to understand what it would take to build a successful, long-term relationship.

BuildASign's philanthropic mission is to positively impact the communities of its customers and it was important that its employees get excited about their support. After a great deal of thought and discussion, what started out as a simple request for a donation became a full-fledged philanthropic effort:

- A monetary donation in the form of discounted product

- Direct financial donations through BuildASign's matching of employee donations

- Approximately 50 employee volunteers participating in the walk itself

- Employee fundraising in the form of a poker tournament to raise money for the walk

The local Austin experience went so well that BuildASign now supports the Leukemia/Lymphoma Society nationally with the same discounted signage. BuildASign credits the Leukemia/Lymphoma Society

with caring about its goals and creating an experience that truly engaged and empowered employees. It provides the ability to have fun
together and make a difference. And the consistency leads employees
to look forward to doing it again, year after year. They have already
repeated for five years.

The Leukemia/Lymphoma Society, meanwhile, receives the financial benefit of reduced cost for event signage. And BuildASign received
nationwide signage business from the Leukemia/Lymphoma Society
and the associated national branding exposure and credibility. The partnership has created a true win-win scenario.

Austaco, an Austin-based fast food holding
company, supports Neighborhood
Longhorns, a group of University of Texas
coaches who mentor over 6,000 kids to help
keep them in school.

Cardinal Health was pleasantly surprised
how passionate employees became about
their philanthropy, organizing a huge silent
auction in conjunction with a large company
meeting that raised $150,000 for Wounded
Warriors and was matched by the Cardinal
Health Foundation.

Jancoa sees the enthusiasm its employees
exhibit when they pull together for charity,
such as for the Mini-Heart Walk or the Go Red
campaign.

P.D. Morrison had a special visit from the
homeowner of the Habitat for Humanity
house they helped fund and build, bringing
them the book One Family at a Time about
the work of the organization.

Right product, right cause. A very simple and straightforward example of what worked well for Elta, a Dallas-based lotion maker, was a product donation to just the right cause. Elta makes lotion with a very high sun protection factor (SPF), so it is highly effective for people with burns. Elta donated lotion to a local summer camp for child burn victims. In Texas, almost all summer camp activities take place outside, so it is critical that the kids' burned skin be totally protected from further damage. The lotion gave them this protection, and the young campers gratefully wrote thank-you letters to the company for its support. You can imagine that it was an easy choice for the company to support this cause again, especially given how well it aligned with its core business purpose of protecting and nurturing skin.

Could have been better. We all make mistakes. This includes philanthropy as well. There are several factors which can result in a less-than-stellar experience. This can include a lack of shared goals, different expectations, and a lack of recognition.

For example, Truepoint Capital, mentioned in Chapter 2, wanted to develop a strategic relationship with a nonprofit that shared its philanthropic vision. Its Philanthropic Mission Statement reads, "We place great value on supporting causes that expand the experiences, skills and knowledge of the next generation — whether through in-kind donations, monetary contributions, or hands-on participation in community events." The company anticipated contributing thought leadership, employee volunteers, and financial support.

Truepoint Capital identified a small nonprofit which seemed to fit the bill. After taking a substantial donation with the promise of further, future engagement with the company, the nonprofit subsequently failed to meet its commitment to a meaningful partnership. Chairman and CEO Michael Chasnoff said, "The experience felt like a transaction rather than the start of a strategic relationship."

Ultimately it was revealed that the nonprofit had significant connections with other brokerage firms, which created a conflict with a Truepoint Capital relationship. The company did not even receive a thank-you note, and the agreed upon plan was never realized. You can imagine that Truepoint Capital is not anxious to repeat this experience and is even more diligent now in scrutinizing potential matches to ensure a lack of potential conflicts.

As it regards devoting leadership time, such as serving on a board of directors, Tillie Hidalgo Lima, President and CEO of Best Upon Request encountered a frustrating situation when the other directors of a board she had agreed to serve on only wanted to continue with the status quo and were afraid to make changes or try new things to advance their results.

Hahn Texas devoted substantial in-kind resources to a nonprofit, only to have the effort go totally unused. Understandably, Hahn, Texas is not looking forward to supporting the organization again.

Even we have experienced a disappointing philanthropy endeavor. We were really proud to be able to make our first donation. While it was not a huge amount, it was significant for us as a new business. Initially, it seemed as though things were going well. We were invited to present our donation at a public event, which we did. However, immediately following the presentation of our check, the Executive Director asked us if we would be interested in sponsoring a table at their large fundraising event. Since we did not have the resources left to do so, we had to decline, which left us feeling deflated rather than excited.

As you think through and document your current giving, consider using the following tool:

TOOL #1: Who Do You Give To?

1. Current philanthropy: What does your business currently do philanthropically?

☐ Provide financial support to nonprofits
☐ Provide matching support of employee contributions
☐ Provide volunteer support by individuals
☐ Provide group volunteer support

If yes, what types of group volunteer activities: _____

_____

☐ Provide free products to nonprofits (*also known as in-kind or pro bono*)
☐ Provide free services to nonprofits (*also known as in-kind or pro bono*)
☐ Run an annual employee giving campaign. If yes, what type of campaign: _____
☐ Nothing yet
☐ Other _____

2. What has motivated your business to give? (*Check all that apply*)

☐ Improve employee attraction and retention
☐ Enhance employee skills
☐ Improve employee teaming
☐ Build brand and corporate image
☐ Increase revenue and market share
☐ Improve the community
☐ Altruism — it is the right thing to do
☐ Support a specific organization or issue. If so, which organization/issue: _____
☐ Other _____

3. On the following chart, list organizations you've given to in the past year:

Nonprofits donated to in the last year	Financial donation, volunteers, or product/service	Amount given	Why the business gave (see reasons above)

Gear-Up Step 2: What causes light your fire? _____

Step two in the gear-up process is to determine what causes spark your passion today, nevermind where you currently give. We all know about the current trend to find your passion and pursue it as your occupation. You will lose yourself in something you love and your work won't even seem like work. So, too, it is with philanthropy. Finding and investing in causes that light your own personal fire (or those of your employees) will be more fulfilling and meaningful than if you just support causes when solicited. And we each light up by different things and for different reasons.

Personal circumstances. One common reason for giving is having lost a loved one to disease or a situation. Hence the many supporters of the American Cancer Society, the American Heart Association, Mothers Against Drunk Drivers, National Center for Missing and Exploited Children, and others. The story is told that Steve Case, Co-Founder of America On-Line (AOL), lost his brother to brain cancer and became an avid supporter of and donor to cancer research. We probably all know someone, perhaps even yourself, with a similar story.

Business alignment. It's no coincidence that Patagonia Founder Yvon Chouinard is committed to protecting the environment; his company's mission, after all, is to equip us for the outdoors. But Chouinard has gone so far as to dedicate 1% of Patagonia's sales to environmental charities. He further co-founded One Percent for the Planet, an alliance that helps small companies pledge to do the same.

Another example, Austin-based National Instruments, makes high-end scientific testing equipment. Not surprisingly, they care deeply about science. So they set out to inspire more kids to pursue careers in engineering and science by sponsoring robotics competitions for teens and pre-teens. Who wouldn't love LEGO robots? They also mentor science, technology, engineering, and math (STEM) students from local schools. As laudable as it is to increase the number STEM students, its employees love the program as well. National Instruments is a mainstay on annual "best places to work" lists and their turnover rate is 50% lower than the industry average.

Aramark is another good example of a company that took the time to identify three core interests to focus on: 1) work force readiness to build critical employment and career skills; 2) basic human services including access to food, clothing and a healthy housing environment; and 3) health and wellness through education and awareness.

These areas align with Aramark's business lines: food service, uniforms and career apparel, and facilities management. So Aramark supports local community centers, Junior Achievement, Big Brothers Big Sisters, and Reading Is Fundamental in order to see results in a select number of chosen causes.

Mike Schaefer, Owner of Seattle-based Soaring Heart Natural Bed, agrees with this methodology. His business's premise is values-driven. More than simply turning a profit, he and his employees want to help people sleep better. Their philanthropy aligns with this purpose. One very successful project uses their raw materials as the basis for volunteering at the local children's hospital to help the kids build their very own customized pillows. The employees love this project and Mike believes the synergy with Soaring Heart's business solidifies philanthropy as part of who they are.

Owner or employee passion. Owners and employees may each have their own opinions about where they would like to give back. Centennial, an executive search firm based in Cincinnati, Ohio encourages employees to volunteer individually, according to their personal passions. Staff members are even allowed time off to pursue their passions. For one employee, the Boy Scouts was his passion. He was helping with the Pinewood Derby, a competition that races handheld wooden cars, homemade by the boys, against each other. He reported that one mother watching the races had tears in her eyes from watching her autistic son, who rarely smiled, beam as his car finished the race. This experience clearly tapped into the interest and excitement of that employee.

The same held true for Tom Siebel, Founder of Siebel Systems, when he became keenly interested in reducing methamphetamine addiction. He was introduced to the problem through a friend in Montana who, as a county sheriff, saw the epidemic first-hand. Siebel funded the Meth Project in Montana, which has since migrated to several other states, helping dramatically reduce methamphetamine use.

We might have a particular soft spot for a certain portion of the population. One Cincinnati acquaintance of mine (Debbie), Judy Harmony, felt strongly that pre-teen girls were a part of the population at serious risk. She felt that offering a gathering place and life skills education tailored to their age and gender could make a tremendous difference to their success in life. So she founded girlzONLY to address this need.

A good way for you (or a group of your employees) to begin is to complete the following tool. This list of causes will prompt you to reflect on specific charitable areas for which you feel a certain affinity. The second list will help you further narrow your focus by identifying certain populations you may feel strongly about supporting.

TOOL #2: What Lights Your Fire?

Even though you or your business may have never donated to some of these causes, please check those in which you have an interest and may want to explore further.

1. In general, what are your broad areas of interest? (*Check all that apply.*)

- ❑ Arts and culture
- ❑ Environment
- ❑ Health
- ❑ Human services
- ❑ Education
- ❑ Animal welfare
- ❑ Disaster relief
- ❑ Scientific and/or technology research
- ❑ Political/social change
- ❑ Poverty
- ❑ Faith/spiritual
- ❑ Human/civic rights
- ❑ Public safety
- ❑ Economic development
- ❑ Preserving cultural heritage
- ❑ Preserving land or species
- ❑ Leadership
- ❑ Other _____

2. If you want to focus on people, are there certain populations in which you have a specific interest? *(Check all that apply.)*

- ❑ Young children (0-5 years)
  - a. Boys
  - b. Girls
- ❑ Children (6-13 years)
  - a. Boys
  - b. Girls
- ❑ Youth (14-21 years)
  - a. Boys
  - b. Girls
- ❑ Adults
- ❑ Elderly (70 years and over)
- ❑ Men
- ❑ Women
- ❑ African-American
- ❑ Hispanic
- ❑ Asian
- ❑ Homeless
- ❑ Gay/Lesbian/Transgender
- ❑ Disabled
- ❑ Immigrants
- ❑ Incarcerated or formerly incarcerated individuals
- ❑ Artists/Musicians
- ❑ Scientists
- ❑ Researchers
- ❑ Entrepreneurs
- ❑ Victims of crime &/or domestic violence
- ❑ Veterans
- ❑ Other _____

Successful Giving, LLC. Adapted from Tracy Gary, *Inspired Philanthropy: Your Step by Step Guide to Creating a Giving Plan and Leaving a Legacy* (2000)

If this tool is too detailed or overwhelming to start with, it may be help-ful to see the popularity of high-level causes for corporations coming from the most recent CECP study:

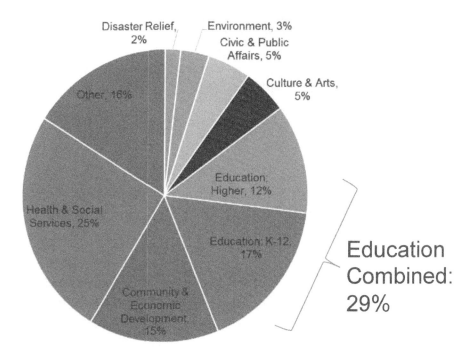

From "Making the Business Case: Trends in Corporate Societal Investment," CECP. http://cecp. co/. Reprinted by permission of CECP.

While education as a whole is the most prevalent category, there are many categories to choose from and, as stated, it is a decision that should be very carefully considered and customized to your particular business.

It might also be helpful to see a different study on causes businesses support, according to the Community Involvement study by the Boston Col-lege Center for Corporate Citizenship:

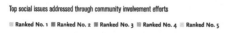

Top social issues addressed through community involvement efforts

Ranked No. 1 Ranked No. 2 Ranked No. 3 Ranked No. 4 Ranked No. 5

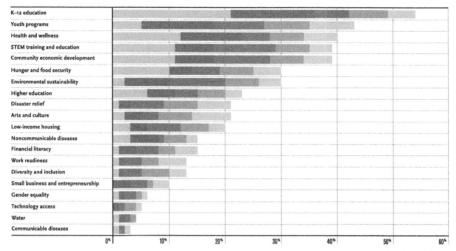

From "Community Involvement Study 2015" ©2015, Boston College Center for Corporate Citizenship. Reproduced with the permission of Boston College Center for Corporate Citizenship.

Regardless of what the rest of the companies are supporting and what the studies above show, the most important decision to make at this point is what cause really grabs your heart, whether by circumstance, business alignment or personal or employee interest, and therefore motivates you to want to improve the situation.

We should additionally point out that, as with any strategy, focusing on a focused few (like Aramark) is much more effective than spreading yourself too thin across many causes. This methodology allows your giving to have much deeper impact through more significant and better thought-out giving. In *The Business of Generosity*, Steven Graves talks about this as being a shift in indiscriminate giving to strategic giving. "Targeting," he says, "has become the name of the game."[64]

Gear-Up Step 3: Creating a culture of giving _____

Creating — and then fostering — a culture of giving is important to the long-term sustainability of a philanthropy program. It is fair to say that support from company executives is a critical success factor. But that's not enough.

Hiring the right people, who want to work for a company that gives back is an imperative for executives and their human resources staff. Without grass roots support, no company can achieve a genuine culture of giving. At best it might be mandated from the top, but it won't be authentic. And the larger the critical mass of employees who appreciate and are proud of your firm for giving back, the more attractive you will be to prospective employees who share those values.

The right people, though, still need to connect with the right opportunity. The Moonridge Group, a Las Vegas-based organization that connects nonprofits and philanthropy and facilitates community-wide initiatives, says that "Everything begins with engagement . . . it's important to start by creating opportunities for fulfilling engagement . . . knowing that once someone volunteers, they often develop a vested interest in supporting that organization into the future."[65]

> Knowledge Sphere, Inc., the business coaching firm mentioned earlier, agrees with building a giving culture. Their staff believe in making philanthropy a widely known core value of the company, which in turn helps attract the right potential employees.
>
> Likewise, Marcia Ballinger, Principal of Keystone Search, a full-service retained search firm out of Minneapolis, Minnesota says the company's commitment to philanthropy brings the "right people to the firm, those who value giving back."

Make your philanthropy explicit in your list of company core values so that current employees and potential hires alike understand the significant commitment you have made to giving back. Then "walk the talk" — give back in all the ways you can on a regular basis so your staff and the rest of the world know you are genuine in your support of the community.

Key points

- Reviewing who you currently give to can be very instructive in planning for the future.

- Taking time to carefully choose which causes to support is time well spent to help ensure enthusiasm for your effort.

- Focus on a few causes rather than too many.

- Create an authentic culture of philanthropy.

6

I is for Identify Your Philanthropy Vision

"It is every man's obligation to put back into the world at least the equivalent of what he takes out of it."

- Albert Einstein, physicist

We know that giving back provides your business with many benefits: it improves employee attraction and retention and enhances their skills, increases revenue and market share, boosts your reputation, improves the community where you and your employees work and live, and affirms the mandate from consumers and businesspeople alike that businesses should support the community. The first step in the process of developing your philanthropy plan is determining what causes you want to support.

Now that you have reviewed both your current giving and desired giving, the next step of the GIVES model is "I": identifying what change you want to see happen in the world and determining exactly how you will go about helping that change come to pass. It's tempting to jump right into donating because — let's face it — the giving is the fun part. But laying a strong foundation of charitable issues you:

➔ most want to support . . .

➔ with objectives you think you can achieve . . .

➔ along with a plan on how you will make decisions and . . .

➔ what types of resources you will give . . .

will ultimately pay off with even stronger meaning and gratification.

As a result, we've devoted the next three chapters to various facets of "I" for Identify. In this chapter, we'll examine setting philanthropic goals. In Chapter 7, we'll learn how to create methodical and sustainable organizational decision-making structures for your philanthropy. Finally, in Chapter 8, we'll explore various options of what to give: money, time, or in-kind donations.

Philanthropic goal-setting

The diagram below from the United Nations Millennium Goals lays out some of the world's most intractable problems at a very high level:

Available at www.un.org/millennialgoals/

From consumers' standpoint, some suggested goals are shown on the following chart from the 2013 Cone Communications/Echo Global CSR Study, which lays out the causes consumers care most about.

THE ONE ISSUE CONSUMERS MOST WANT COMPANIES TO ADDRESS

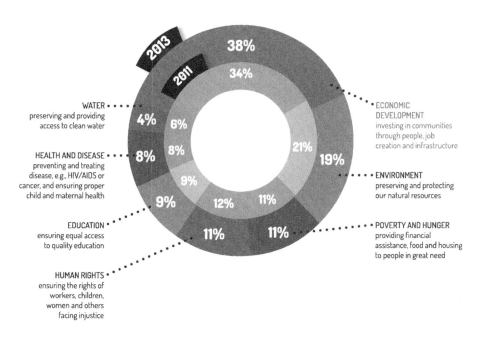

WATER
preserving and providing
access to clean water

HEALTH AND DISEASE
preventing and treating
disease, e.g., HIV/AIDS or
cancer, and ensuring proper
child and maternal health

EDUCATION
ensuring equal access
to quality education

HUMAN RIGHTS
ensuring the rights of
workers, children,
women and others
facing injustice

ECONOMIC
DEVELOPMENT
investing in communities
through people, job
creation and infrastructure

ENVIRONMENT
preserving and protecting
our natural resources

POVERTY AND HUNGER
providing financial
assistance, food and housing
to people in great need

From 2013 Cone Communications / Echo Global CSR Study, http://conecomm.com/. Reprinted by permission of Cone Communications.

These lists of ideas represent only a few of the myriad possibilities. The key to creating your own goals is to reflect on your favorite causes and carefully think through aspirational targets for change. This process should balance both being realistic with not setting your sights too low. In other words, be appropriately aggressive with your goals.

One seemingly unrealistic goal is the focus of some nonprofits: world peace. Youth exchange organizations like American Field Service (AFS) and Children's International Summer Village (CISV) are working toward this end by teaching participants to appreciate cultural differences and helping them build friendships around the world. Their hope is that in so doing, contentiousness, discord, and the risk of future conflict will decrease.

Nonprofit scan

If the United Nations or CONE study charts do not provide a goal you can get excited about, it might be helpful to peruse a list of nonprofits to see if one of their missions, at a very specific level, enthuses you. That specific cause will roll up into a more general area.

For example, Emancipet in Austin, Texas focuses on spaying and neutering dogs and cats, addressing the root cause of pet overpopulation. The more general area in this case is "animal welfare." The more specific cause is "pet sterilization."

If you are looking for a list of humanitarian organizations, the following on-line sites offer information about nonprofits. These sites will be discussed in more detail in Chapter 9, but they are laid out here to give you ideas of nonprofit causes:

- www.charitynavigator.org

- www.guidestar.org

- www.bbb.org/us/wise-giving

- www.charitywatch.org

- http://givewell.org

Community resources

Many cities also have their own versions of information repositories about nonprofits. In most communities, the local United Way serves as a key resource. In Austin (where the authors live) there are many examples of philanthropy resources, several of which are listed. Though these organizations are not specifically set up to help you determine your giving goals, they are resources that provide information about the good work going on in the community:

- **Little Helping Hands** connects families with volunteer opportunities so they are well-versed in the human power needs of nonprofits.

- **Volunteer Spot** enables firms to streamline the management of their volunteering.

- **A Legacy of Giving** encourages young people to get involved in philanthropy.

- **I Live Here I Give Here** encourages giving of all kinds, both individual and corporate, and sponsors a community-wide giving day, Amplify Austin, each year.

- **Austin Gives** specifically focuses on promoting and recognizing business philanthropy.

- **The United Way** supported database and hotline, 211, provides information on social service resources.

- **Keep Austin Generous** and **Give As You Get** provide giving platforms for both business and personal giving.

Nonprofit organizations should clearly outline their mission statements on their website, so you should be able to easily discern which ones are organizations that address an issue in which you are interested. Suffice it to say, there is no lack of resources to help you identify your giving goals.

"Million Dollar Visioning"

If you are still having difficulty developing your goals, you can employ the Million Dollar Visioning tool that was developed by Tracy Gary in her book

Inspired Philanthropy to help you dream big because it lets you "play rich." The questions in the tool will prompt you to think more deeply about the possibilities, which will in turn hopefully inspire you to lock in on a goal or multiple goals that truly motivate you to action.

TOOL #3: Million Dollar Visioning

1. From the list of broad areas of interest you care about (completed in the What Lights Your Fire? exercise), choose one problem in society you would like to help resolve:

2. Now imagine you have just been given $1,000,000 to invest in solving that problem, with no strings attached. What is your action plan?

   • What change strategy would you employ?

   • What would you do?

   • Who would you convene or hire to support your efforts?

   • What institutional partners would you choose?

   • What outcomes would you hope for and in what time frame?

   • How would you be involved to maximize impact?

   • How would you share your vision with others?

3. What is holding you back from starting some of this work, even without $1,000,000?

- Adapted from Inspired Philanthropy by Tracy Gary (2008).

Use this exercise to reflect on your vision of how you or your business would give money away to help create the world you want. Even if you cannot answer all of the questions, let the introspection they stimulate guide your thinking towards developing your goal, especially the outcomes you hope to achieve.

Change strategies

Hopefully, by the time you have completed this suggested research, you will find a sweet spot for investing your resources. One other tool in the goal-setting process may also be useful in identifying your action plans. While not intended to be comprehensive, this list of possible strategies to accomplish positive change toward your causes of choice may jumpstart your creative energies toward developing your goals:

TOOL #4: Possible Change Strategies

Advocacy
- Influencing public policy
- Legal reform

Capacity building and leadership training

Coalition building

Demonstrating

Disaster relief

Economic development

Education, training or resource development

Fundraising

Electoral politics
- Supporting candidates and initiatives
- Voter education and registration

Grassroots community organizing

Media and media reform

Meditation or prayer

Research
- Problem analysis
- Solution analysis

Systems change

- ©2010, Successful Giving, LLC.

Documenting your plans _____

Once you have locked in on a few goals you are committing to achieving with your philanthropy, document them on Tool #5 below, Philanthropic Goal Setting.

For example, the Chairman and CEO of Kimberly-Clark says, "At Kimberly-Clark, we make our vision to lead the world in essentials for a better life a reality by building a sustainable enterprise. For us that means delivering consistent growth as well as creating a strong culture and being committed to corporate social responsibility."

And Michael Dell, Chairman and CEO of Dell, says this about the goal of the company's 2020 "Legacy of Good" plan: "The changes headed our way require more than incremental progress. They demand meaningful, systemic change and, for businesses, that starts with a new mindset about corporate responsibility. We have to look beyond our walls to inspire sustainable practices throughout our entire ecosystem, making sustainability easier for our customers and partners."[66]

Personally, for our business, Successful Giving, our goal is to see more resources of all types flow into the community from businesses: financial, volunteerism, and donated products or services.

TOOL #5: Philanthropic Goal-Setting

What are three differences in the world that you and your business could positively impact through your philanthropy?

1. _____

2. _____

3. _____

- ©2010, Successful Giving, LLC.

Creating a philanthropic mission statement _____

The last exercise in this section helps you hone your thoughts, based on your newly established goals, into a concise statement that will guide all of your philanthropy. Hopefully the work you did to spend your million dollars or the list of possible change strategies allowed you to already start developing your action plans. While it can be more comfortable to stay at the 50,000 foot level, you will not advance your cause and affect change if you cannot convert these ideas into a concrete plan of action.

TOOL #6: What Do You Want to Happen?

A **giving mission statement** is a short statement (generally no more than three sentences) that identifies:

1. Who will be engaged in the philanthropy outlined in the mission statement? (e.g, Baker Industries)

2. What values guide this statement? (e.g, ensuring equal access)

3. What issues or organizations will be targeted? (e.g. the arts)

4. What basic strategy or actions will be used to help resolve the issue? (e.g., by donating 2% of our income, allowing employees to volunteer and donating computer equipment)

5. Timeframe for action and review (including who is responsible for the review)

- ©2010, Successful Giving, LLC.

As with the Million Dollar Visioning exercise, you do not need to fill in every blank if you have not yet made all of the associated decisions nor does the statement have to be extensive. Making it concise is a good exercise in focus and ensuring that you consolidate your ideas to a few steps you can realistically take toward making the change happen. For a business, the statement should also serve to mobilize your employees around your chosen causes.

Using the template above, you might end up with something that reads like this: *Baker Industries will focus on ensuring equal access to the arts by donating 2% of net income, allowing employees to volunteer twice a year at the Children's Museum, and donating computer equipment. We will do this for the next 12 months and review our progress at a company meeting in October.*

Business mission statements can and should vary greatly to match the business' focus. Here are a few more examples of companies' mission statements:

Example #1:
We seek to reduce the amount of violence within families in the community. We do this through the following actions:

- *donating money to family violence prevention programs;*

- *volunteering 10 hours per month on parent telephone hotlines that seek to reduce stress in families;*

- *continuing our 10-year commitment as a Big Brother/Big Sister; and*

- *advocating for laws that crack down on crimes of violence against families and that protect victims of violence.*

These actions will continue to be our priority for the next three years.

Example #2:

We believe that nothing can positively affect a person's life more than a good education. Therefore, we devote whatever extra money and time we have to helping students get scholarships and access to the best educational opportunities available. For the next three years, we will specifically help 20 high school students each year obtain the scholarships they need to continue their education.

Example #3:

Our firm believes in libraries and literacy as a means of strengthening the community. We will contribute to libraries and reading programs, especially those that are bilingual and that bring the community together. During the next five years, we will fund 20% of the costs of our community's English as a Second Language program through the local libraries.

Cardinal Health, a healthcare provider in Columbus, Ohio, is a great example of a business that has given tremendous thought and energy to its philanthropic mission. Because it is in the healthcare business, it is not surprising that its goals center on health. Its mission is two-fold:

1. Increase healthcare efficiency and effectiveness; and

2. Reduce prescription drug abuse

Cardinal Health has been able to make significant progress towards its mission by being very clear about its focus and by taking action on each of these two issues (see more in Chapter 10).

Standard Heating, another firm we know from Minneapolis, Minnesota, has a very different and more open-ended mission: to leverage its heating, ventilation, and air conditioning (HVAC) resources to help the community. The focus is not on certain causes but rather on using its own organizational capacity for good, wherever those opportunities may arise.

So when a local military serviceman bought a home that needed significant renovation in order to be livable, Standard Heating stepped in to help when he was deployed to the Middle East before he could finish the home's rehabilitation. Employees finished the HVAC work on the home so that the family could move in immediately and finish the rest of the renovation over time. Actions like these help the company fulfill its mission to use its offerings and experience to do good.

Key points

- Take time to establish your vision of what you want to happen as a result of your philanthropy. Remember, those who fail to plan, plan to fail.

- There are many resources to help with ideas: nonprofits themselves, community resources, and tools to help you think through your goal setting.

- Documenting your mission in a concise statement will keep you focused and your employees energized.

I is for Identify Your Philanthropy Decision-Making

7

> "As I started getting rich, I started thinking, 'What the hell am I going to do with all this money? You have to learn to give."
>
> - Ted Turner, media mogul and philanthropist

Hopefully, by this time you know how giving back will benefit your employees, your business, and your community; you've identified what causes enthuse you; and you've developed and documented your philanthropy mission statement. Now it is time to create a decision process for your philanthropy.

Each firm should develop its own unique plan for how philanthropy decisions are made within the company. Some executives want a strong hand and even ultimate decision-making authority in these decisions, while other firms prefer an employee-led, very democratic style of decision-making regarding giving.

In the sections that follow, we'll explore a few of the determinations to be made regarding *how* you make your philanthropy decisions.

Decision-making structure _____

There are five options for structures that you can use to make your philanthropy decisions:

1. **Foundation.** One option is to create a foundation that takes in all donations and redistributes them to nonprofits via an application process. Most typically, nonprofits complete these applications, which describe how they will use the requested resources. The foundation then makes grants to the selected nonprofits over a timeframe, typically from one to three years. Business foundations will usually develop guidelines for the causes they will and will not support and make this publicly available (generally on their websites) to guide nonprofits that are thinking of applying for grants.

    A good example of a company that uses this type of arrangement is Bazaarvoice, a consumer input firm located in Austin, Texas that helps businesses use technology to connect with their customers' feedback. The Bazaarvoice Foundation started as a grassroots movement at the headquarters location that stemmed from a company culture based on generosity. Says Bazaarvoice Co-Founder Brett Hurt, "We started to discuss what type of soul we would like this new person — this new collective that we were founding named Bazaarvoice — to have. We wanted that soul to be a generous one. We wanted that soul to engage the entirety of Bazaarvoice and, most importantly, its employees."

    The community impact created by this organic passion over the years led the leadership team to formalize the company's commitment to generosity by seeding and registering the Bazaarvoice Foundation as a 501(c)3 just prior to the company's 2012 IPO. In this case, employees are integrally involved in running the foundation and in its decision making. At its formation, Bazaarvoice leaders had employees gather to choose the mission for the newly formalized foundation, knowing they wanted it to focus on a single area that both embodied the spirit of their employees and offered the opportunity to make a deep, measurable impact on the communities they call home.

A group of the staff, who embodied the core company value of generosity, organized opportunities for volunteering, fundraising drives, and other ways to give back, taking care that employees had plenty of options for involvement. And they continue to involve employees by having them vote on which nonprofits receive support. Not all foundations involve employees in such a robust way, but Bazaarvoice felt strongly about having its people at the table for these decisions.

If not employees, many foundations rely on a board of directors to make giving decisions. If you decide to start a foundation, in fact, you will be bound by certain federal regulations — including establishing a board of directors and making a minimum 5% annual distribution of the corpus. There are many who believe that unless you have at least $5 million or more in funding for a foundation, you may want to consider either a donor-advised fund (DAF) with your local community foundation or giving directly from your business.

2. **Philanthropy teams.** Another popular form of decision-making is through a philanthropy team. This type of team often includes employees from each part of the company, by function or division, so that all employee interests are represented. The team then comes together on a fairly regular basis (usually monthly or quarterly) to look at possible organizations to support and decides which will receive resources. Keep in mind that many times employee teams not only make financial funding decisions, but also determine where employee volunteers might be deployed and where in-kind products or services might be donated.

For example, Truepoint Capital has a series of philanthropic committees, made up of both permanent and rotating members, which meet regularly to review charitable opportunities and decide which ones will receive support. Its philanthropy effort includes three categories of committees:

- *Employee*: supports individual employee involvement and fosters firm-wide team building

- *Client*: supports client involvement in nonprofits

- *Firm-wide*: supports collective vision of Truepoint Capital

Each team has a different decision-making body most closely aligned with the content of the category. Team members include both those whose primary function relates most closely to the group as well as those for whom their individual interest makes them a good match. Philanthropy is so important to Truepoint that the annual corporate report includes a full two-page spread devoted to highlighting the company's community involvement.

In a slightly different way of involving employees, Keystone Search feels strongly that while commitment to philanthropy must come from the top, its deployment is better served by spreading out the decision making. So its partners have their own allocation and each decides where their own amount goes. Non-partner staff members also get their own allocation to give away as a group.

In my (Debbie) time at AT&T and Lucent Technologies, I found that my employees really loved being involved in the decisions around philanthropy. We made it a priority to arrange our business so that we could allow some time off for these philanthropy decision-making meetings.

3. **Staff-chosen.** Staff-chosen philanthropy is distinguished from team-chosen in that it gives all staff members, not just a representative group, a chance to provide input. To involve all employees in the company's philanthropic decisions, most companies will choose to gather employee preferences via a survey or other mass mechanism. However, the challenge of giving each employee their say is in providing sufficient information to help them make an informed decision.

Nevertheless, most people like being asked for their opinion so this type of decision making usually helps foster a high percentage of employee engagement and tends to boost employee morale.

As an example, Convio, an Austin-based provider of customer relationship management software (which has now merged with Blackbaud), had an annual grants program. This program funded 10 nonprofits each year, each of which was nominated and voted on by all Convio employees. Former CEO Gene Austin feels that while commitment to philanthropy must be driven from the top, widespread employee involvement, along with organized company volunteering, established a competitive differentiator for the company in attracting and retaining employees. It also created a strong culture of organizational pride.

4. **Executive-chosen.** Some companies prefer to consolidate the power for these types of decisions in the executive suite — especially if the main reason for giving back is to enhance the corporate brand, increase revenue, or align their business with their philanthropy. The senior team most likely has the best grasp of the strategic implications of their choices. On the other hand, if your employees are the main impetus for your giving, keeping the decisions solely to the executives may be disenfranchising.

    As a cautionary tale, Rob Solomon, CEO of Bulldog Solutions, learned that lesson the hard way. His first volunteer effort was a cause near and dear to his heart. However, when volunteer day came, hardly any staff members showed up to support the effort. He learned that employee input was critical to successful volunteer deployment, as well as having a clear value proposition for employees to participate. Says Rob, "Grassroots involvement is critical. It should NOT be done for the recognition but instead for the staff and because it's the right thing to do." Since his change to employee-driven decisions, a full two-thirds of his staff are involved in the community.

    On the other hand, Rachel Clemens, President of Creative Suitcase, uses executive decision-making in a very effective way. Each year, she chooses one nonprofit project that will receive a donation valued at 5% of Creative Suitcase's profits. Because all of the company's philanthropic focus is on one effort, it is critical that it be strategically the best opportunity for her firm. As President, Rachel is in the best position to make that call. You may recall that by using the project to create memorable holiday marketing pieces, she not only helps her company brand but also energizes her employees — they love it!

5. **Client-chosen.** Other companies choose to use their philanthropy as an opportunity to involve their clients, which serves the secondary purpose: letting clients know about the company's generosity. Customer involvement increases social impact by potentially broadening engagement, improving education, expanding giving, and increasing the company's bottom line through greater company and product loyalty.

   A few relatively recent examples of nationwide customer-driven philanthropy include the Pepsi Refresh Project, which awarded a total of $20 million in grants to customer-recommended social impact projects; State Farm's Cause An Effect, a youth-led crowd-sourced philanthropic project that administered a $5 million fund; and American Express's Members Project, which allowed individuals to suggest and vote on projects, directing more than $5 million of corporate philanthropy.[67]

   Another example, Plante Moran, a financial advisory company from Cincinnati, Ohio, allocates fully half of its philanthropy budget to causes of client interest (the other half is decided by an employee committee). Clients make requests for Plante Moran's support of their favorite philanthropy projects and the managing partner of the office makes the funding decisions. This methodology works well when a company has a limited number of significant clients.

   Other businesses let all of their customers provide input on the decision about where donations are made. Give Something Back, a business office supply company mentioned earlier, allocates 100% of its profits to the community across all of its offices. Clients making purchases are sent a ballot (as are employees from that store) from which to select their choice of nonprofits. The donations are then based on the percentages of votes for each nonprofit, which results

in a wide diversity of supported charities and tends to promote customer loyalty because of their inclusion in the process.

Door Number 3 also tries to find philanthropic projects that
both their staff and clients love so as to be a "home run for everyone," says past President M.P. Mueller.

And, of course, a mix of the various approaches described above is also
an option. For example, Centennial, a personnel search firm located in Cincinnati, Ohio, uses a blended approach. Employees can suggest nonprofits
they are passionate about for funding; the executives ultimately make the
decision, based on employee lobbying along with their determination of
what gifts will have the biggest impact on the business.

As another example, Austin-based Hanger, Inc., the nation's leading
patient-care provider and distributor of orthotic, prosthetic, and rehabilita-
tive solutions, created an internal "giving committee." The committee intentionally comprises employees from across the country who represent
all facets of the company and its business units. The committee vets and
evaluates grant requests and provides recommendations on funding certain nonprofits and projects to their foundation's board, which gives the
final approval.

And Truepoint Capital intentionally divides its philanthropy decisions
into two distinct aspects:

- Employees bring forward requests for support, and

- Clients also request support of favorite projects

In this way, it intentionally involves the two most important stakeholder groups, clients and employees, in the process. To get a sense for what
resources other companies on average utilize, look at the chart on the next
page from Boston College. As you choose a decision-making body or person
for your organization, make sure that it best fits *your* business strategy and
the reason for *your* philanthropy.

Perspectives companies consider to prioritize issues

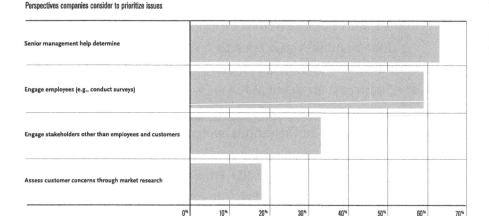

From "Community Involvement Study 2015" ©2015 Boston College Center for Corporate Citizenship, Reproduced with the permission of Boston College Center for Corporate Citizenship.

Decision criteria

It is important to establish this criteria upfront so that you have a tool for comparing all of the opportunities competing for donations of your money and other resources. Identifying your criteria beforehand not only makes the evaluation more even-handed and fair for the potential recipients, but also keeps the decision makers focused on the most important factors. Having established criteria also helps to avoid making decisions a popularity contest or basing them predominately (or solely!) on emotion.

Chapter 9, "V is for Vet," will discuss how to make decisions about which specific nonprofits receive your funding. This process is known as "vetting" and will include more about criteria that can be used during the decision.

Frequency of decisions

Many organizations tie their philanthropy to the fiscal year, so they decide their donations annually. Other companies find that annual decisions do not allow enough flexibility to support opportunities that come up during the year. In these cases, many firms opt for quarterly decisions so that they can make gifts throughout the year. Infrequently we see companies opt for making decisions each month in order to be the most timely and responsive to nonprofit requests for funding.

The frequency of philanthropy decision making should reflect the firm's choice and, in part, be based on how often it is practical for decision makers to gather and make time for their serious consideration. If company financials including cash flow are highly varied throughout the year, this too may have an impact on how often decisions are made.

Previously mentioned Hanger, Inc. established a philanthropy plan that incorporates formal quarterly application and funding cycles in addition to the flexibility to fund smaller "pop-up" opportunities outside of these cycles.

How will you make decisions?

Decision making takes several forms and should dovetail with who will make the decision. If you have one executive or individual making the giving decision, your decisions will be unilateral and will not need further definition of the methodology. The decision maker will consider the options for funding, using established decision criteria, and make a decision.

On the other hand, if you have any kind of group involved, you will need to choose a decision methodology: 1) democratic or 2) consensus. A democratic process of voting will result in the top vote getter winning the company's support. On the other hand, some firms prefer that teams work until they can come to consensus — that all team members can support the decision. This methodology usually takes longer to arrive at the decision but ultimately may have richer support from across the team.

Logistics

Logistics for decision-making will also be based on the decision owner. If a single decision maker will make all decisions, the logistics are irrelevant. If a group is involved, the logistics most likely will be driven by the geographic proximity of the team. If the whole team is physically located in the same building or city, face-to-face meetings are a good choice to allow for most effective team building and communication. If the group is spread across the country or the world, it is more practical to have meetings via telephone, video, or web conference.

Hanger, Inc. is again a good example of a company that has thought through the logistics to ensure geographically dispersed teams can be involved in scheduled philanthropic decision-making via audio and video conferencing networks. This arrangement makes it easiest for the team members to fully participate.

We strongly recommend establishing the decision-making elements dicussed above upfront so that the process flows smoothly once it is begun. The tool on the following page can be used as a foundation for developing your own decision matrix. You can also find more information and tools in Chapter 9 for vetting organizations and identifying the best partners for your philanthropic efforts.

TOOL #7: Decision-Making	
Who will make your philanthropy decisions?	☐ Foundation ☐ Philanthropy Team ☐ Employees ☐ Executives ☐ Clients/Customers
Who can make requests for donations?	☐ Employees ☐ Executives/Owners ☐ Clients/Customers ☐ Organizations can make a request through a formal process (such as RFP) or a website ☐ Organizations can make an unsolicited request
How often will you make philanthropy decisions?	☐ Annually ☐ Semi-Annually ☐ Quarterly ☐ Monthly ☐ As needed
How will you make philanthropy decisions?	☐ Democratic/vote ☐ Consensus
How will you meet?	☐ Face-to-face ☐ Via technology (audio, video, web conference)

Key points _____

- The decision making process and owner should be unique to your business and what works best for you. It can range from just one executive making all decisions to employee groups, clients, or combinations thereof.

- It is important to establish criteria by which you will make your giving decisions in order to be consistent and best aligned with your plans.

I is for Identify Your Philanthropy Giving

8

"Success unshared is failure."

- John Paul DeJoria, businessman and philanthropist

We know about the many benefits of giving back, including employee advantages, business benefits, and community enhancements. You have identfied causes to support and developed both a mission statement and a decision-making process that will guide your philanthropy. Now it's time to ask: exactly *what* will you give back?

Your methods of giving are limited only by your imagination. But there are three categories of giving typically most appropriate for businesses:

1. Financial
2. Volunteering
3. Donating products or services (also known as *in-kind* or *pro bono* gifting)

Dan Graham, Co-Founder and CEO of BuildASign, debunks the myth "Don't worry about giving back until you're bigger" by encouraging a company to give what it can from the start — whichever of the three methods listed above is appropriate. He says, "Giving back to the community is the right thing to do, no matter what size company you have. Don't have cash to donate? Get the team together and donate your professional skills to a nonprofit who needs the expertise, mentor a child, or help build a house for a deserving family. Every business should think about what positive impact their team can make, and as your company grows, that core value will stay ingrained in your corporate DNA."[68]

AT&T and Lucent Technologies, where I (Debbie) worked, were obviously very large and so could give back in all three ways. For example, one year we sponsored the AT&T/Cincinnati Ballet Fun Run, a financial commitment. That year we also donated a telephone system to the National Underground Railroad Freedom Center, which was still in the early stages of developing the concept of what would eventually become a full-fledged history museum, inspiring future freedom fighters. And we volunteered resources to support the United Way fundraising campaign.

The chart below categorizes giving similarly, though it adds employee gifts to the equation. (Although facilitated by business, employee donations are still essentially *personal* philanthropy — and as such not the focus of this book.) You can see the relative amounts that make up each category, with cash, at 66%, representing the largest percentage of giving:

Employee Time and Contributions Account for 23% of the Value Created by the Average Company

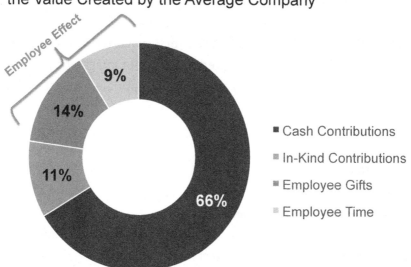

- Cash Contributions
- In-Kind Contributions
- Employee Gifts
- Employee Time

From Emerging Trends in Corporate Contributions, CECP. https://www.michiganfoundations.org. Reprinted by permission of CECP.

The Committee Encouraging Corporate Philanthropy (CECP) advises, "Nonprofits rely on consistent cash funding to pay overhead costs and expand important services, so cash contributions are always in high demand. At the same time, products and professional services are also valuable to nonprofit partners. Companies often have the expertise and resources necessary to provide such important in-kind resources at scale."[69]

So, for example, a garden center business might decide to support the development of an urban garden in a community park:

- Volunteering to clean up the park, prepare the soil and plant the garden

- Donating the fertilizer and plants

- Paying for the incremental watering needed to maintain healthy plants

- Paying for the development of a farmers market to sell the produce and/or flowers to families who otherwise would find it hard to access fresh produce

This community investment might result in providing healthier foods at a lower cost to the surrounding residents, and the investment takes the form of all three types of donations: money, volunteers, and donated product and service.

Financial donations

Cash is king for nonprofits, and they will love you for your monetary donations. Cash provides them maximum flexibility to support operating expenses, program funding, capital expenditures — anything needing payment with money. Nonprofits also often use private donations as leverage for governmental grants, which often require some type of private match in order to receive the government funds.

You may have heard the expression that we should give our "time, talent, and treasure." This method would be equivalent to giving "treasure." Interestingly, almost all of the businesses we talked with have been surprised that they really didn't miss the money they have been giving.

Another growing trend is "B Corporations" (also known as social entrepreneurship), companies that include a specific financial giving component as part of their business model. Previously-mentioned Boston-based Keeper Springs is this type of business, giving away 100% (yes, 100%!) of its profits to help protect our waterways. Bobby Kennedy, Jr. along with his partner Chris Bartle, donate all their time to the cause, paying only their staff of five before giving away all of their earnings to organizations devoted to our water environment. Sacramento's Give Something Back, also mentioned earlier, has the same model — 100% of profits go to charity — but, in its case, the funds are distributed to multiple causes based on client and employee vote.

Buffie Blesi, President of Knowledge Sphere, feels that the capacity to make money is a gift, so giving some of it away — even if just in the form of cash — is called for since the company has been blessed enough to be prosperous.

There are myriad ways to donate financially, including (among others) cash, stock, microloans, venture funding, workplace giving, foundations, and sponsorships. We'll briefly examine the major considerations for each type of financial donation.

Restricted gifts. It is possible to restrict cash gifts to what you want the money spent on. This limitation is less desirable for the nonprofit but allows you as the donor to make sure your cash donations are spent on what you intend.

For example, you may restrict your donation to only pay for current year program operating expenses rather than capital expenditures, which generally pay for buildings or infrastructure.

On the other hand, another example of a restricted gift — especially if you want to support the long-term sustainability of an organization — is to give money to an endowment fund. This generally allows the interest from the asset to be spent each year, but none of the principle.

Because of this, your gift remains intact from year to year and, thanks to the interest provided, saves the nonprofit from continuously having to raise funds, only to repeat the process year after year.

Scholarships. Another example where funds are given but restricted is a scholarship. This form of giving is used to sponsor a certain number of participants through a program, such as underprivileged kids through summer camp or children who cannot otherwise afford it through a program such as The First Tee (www.thefirsttee.org).

Minneapolis-based Keystone Search has had a very rewarding experience with this type of giving by funding underserved students from the most disadvantaged local neighborhoods to go to a private school. Marcia Ballinger, the company's Principal, says, "It is extraordinarily gratifying to watch kids rise from hopelessness to role models for their neighborhood."

M.P. Mueller of Door Number 3 has had a similar experience with the Hispanic Scholarship Consortium, funding scholarships for students as well as for skill development.

Stock. A form of future monetary donation is stock in your company. Many times start-ups who have not yet gone public will gift some stock which becomes valuable only after the initial public offering (IPO) so it represents future and possibly significant money for the nonprofit.

The Entrepreneurs Foundation of Central Texas, based in Austin, facilitates this type of giving. Early-stage companies use this foundation to make stock donations which will have future value if and when they go public. The Entrepreneurs Foundation also facilitates volunteering opportunities for the young employees in these early stage firms who love collaborative hands-on work. This option offers a great way for busy entrepreneurs to be intentionally philanthropic without incurring a significant immediate financial drain.

Microloans. An increasingly popular form of financial giving is microloans. Grameen Bank Founder (and Nobel Prize winner) Mohammed Yunus made this form of funding popular because it is proving to be very empowering and potentially life-changing for the recipients. This movement began with an experiment by Yunus, then a Bangladeshi economics professor. Using his own money, he first lent the equivalent of $26 to a group of 42 workers.

Unlike most commercial loans, no collateral is required and the payback period is usually very short (6-12 months). For example, one woman was able to borrow $50 to buy chickens and sell their eggs. As the chickens reproduced, she could sell more eggs and eventually some of the chicks, enabling her to repay the loan.

The system is based on the notion that the poor have perennially under-utilized skills. The group-based credit program utilizes peer pressure to help ensure borrowers follow through to repay their loans and use discipline in their financial affairs. Interestingly, the overwhelming majority (98%) of borrowers were women.

The women used the profits to send their children to school, improve their families' living conditions and nutrition, and expand their businesses. So the impact was not limited to their own families but to whole communities.

Based on the success of this initial experiment, this form of microcredit gained momentum when Yunus launched the Grameen Bank Project in late 1983 to explore the possibility of offering a broader credit delivery system to provide banking services to the rural poor. Today, most social justice scholars consider microfinance to be one proven tool for fighting poverty on a large scale. (Some microloan programs even include social services such as basic healthcare to help improve loan recipients' living conditions.)

Venture funding. Venture funding is a common tool for funding start-up businesses in the corporate world and is now finding a place among nonprofits. Investors typically donate not only funds but expertise as well to help ensure that the nonprofit succeeds.

One such organization that facilitates this type of funding in Austin, Texas is Mission Capital, which is a merger of Innovation + and Greenlights. This reasonably new venture fund-type arrangement identifies high growth potential nonprofits who are clearly proving to have an impact in the community. It then invests human and financial capital to help them scale much more quickly than they could without such support for a near-term transformational impact.

College Forward was the first nonprofit "community partner" selected out of 40 nominations to participate in this initiative. Innovation + played the role of adviser, mentor, and connector. As such, it made significant contributions of time and energy in addition to strategic capital investments.

As a result, College Forward grew from serving just over 2,000 high school and college students in Austin to over 4,500 students in Central Texas and the Houston area in just two years. Perhaps as importantly, it just secured its first fee-for-service contract to provide college success services for a Houston-based college. This new service positions College Forward for enhanced sustainability because it establishes an earned revenue model that is scalable. And the lives of thousands of low-income, first generation college students are being changed through the success of this program.

Give Something Back has also dabbled in loaning money to nonprofits on occasion, for the right opportunity. An inner city youth organization needed funds to buy a building and Give Something Back decided to depart from its usual client- and employee-decided giving strategy to loan the nonprofit the needed money. This experience went well and the loan was successfully repaid.

Workplace giving campaigns. Businesses have been conducting employee giving campaigns for years, most notably through the United Way of America. The United Way and other similar organizations then ensure the donations either go to the nonprofit of the donor's choice or, more typically, to worthy projects affecting large numbers of people in the community. Variations on this theme have sprung up in more recent years such as Earth Shares, which gives the donated money to environmental causes. This type of giving is very beneficial to employees who want to give back to the community but want to let someone else (i.e. the United Way) research the best recipients for the donations.

A unique twist on workplace giving is for employees to prompt giving directly to a chosen cause. For example, BuildASign agreed to donate $25 for each male employee who participated in "Movember," a nationwide program where men grow facial hair during the month of November to be shaved at the end of the month. Proceeds from this activity go toward prostate cancer awareness. They even involved women who wore fuzzy pink mustaches, which garnered a $10 donation (called Mo Sistas). The employees had fun participating while the company donated to a worthwhile cause that their employees could support.

Employee matching programs. Many businesses have now developed matching programs in which the company will match charitable employee donations, whether dollar-for-dollar or at some percentage. Most typically, a company will match employee contributions to any 501 (c) 3 up to a certain amount such as, for example, $5,000 per year. Some companies restrict their matches to certain causes chosen by the company, such as education-related nonprofits or animal welfare.

Fortune 500 companies have been matching employee donations for many years, but smaller businesses such as BuildASign are now starting to explore this method of giving back as well.

An interesting twist on matching is provided by Cardinal Health, which matches donations of teams who raise money as a group. When a group of employees raised $150,000 for Wounded Warriors, they were able to turn that donation into $300,000 through the company's gift-matching program.

Likewise, CLEAResult, an energy company in Austin, matched employee donations to victims of Haiti's devastating hurricane in 2008. When Hurricane Katrina destroyed much of New Orleans, the company also donated building materials and staff time to help rebuild the city.

The chart on the next page shows the popularity of these employee contribution programs:

86% of Companies Encourage Employee Contributions by Offering At Least One of the Following Matching-Gift Policies

Percentage of Companies Offering...

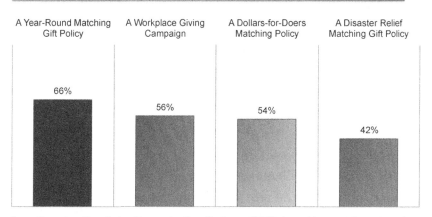

| A Year-Round Matching Gift Policy | A Workplace Giving Campaign | A Dollars-for-Doers Matching Policy | A Disaster Relief Matching Gift Policy |

66%   56%   54%   42%

From Emerging Trends in Corporate Contributions, CECP, https://www.michiganfoundations. org. Reprinted by permission of CECP.

Most matching is generally done for monetary donations by the employee but, as a different type of matching, The Microsoft Store matches employee volunteer hours with a financial donation. For each volunteer hour worked, The Microsoft Store donates $17 to the associated nonprofit. Commonly called "dollars for doers," this matching can also take the form of grants to nonprofits where individuals or teams of employees volunteer. In this case, the grant is a pre-determined amount rather than paid based on a specific amount of hours volunteered. In any case, the nonprofit benefits doubly by receiving monetary donations in addition to sweat equity in the form of a volunteer workforce.

Foundations. As mentioned earlier, a business can also create a foundation to serve as its giving arm. These separate organizations become their own nonprofits and are then able to accept donations from both the company and directly from its employees (representing a tax deductible gift for both).

Most business foundations, in turn, donate to other nonprofits through a formal grant process or more informally through employee nominations. Bazaarvoice, the consumer feedback firm mentioned earlier, is a good example of a company that started its own foundation in order to fund programming which catalyzes highly educated, entrepreneurial low-income youth.

Hanger, Inc., also mentioned earlier, is another example of a company that established its own foundation. Hanger's heritage of charitable giving dates back to the company's founding in 1861. For many years, Hanger clinicians and employees consistently and generously donated millions of dollars in free care and financial contributions to a variety of causes, including hardship cases in their own communities.

In 2009, Hanger formalized and increased its philanthropic work by establishing a nonprofit organization that brought relief in the form of both money and volunteers to Haiti following the devastating earthquake, providing free prosthetic care to more than 1,200 Haitian amputees, and establishing a training program to educate local Haitians to become prosthetic practitioners and technicians for the provision of long-term care in Haiti.

The Hanger Charitable Foundation has made significant progress since its inception, undergoing a name change in 2014 and putting a more formalized structure in place to identify and support causes that are synergistic with the company mantra of "Empowering Human Potential." With a mission to support nonprofit organizations that help people with physical challenges live life as fully as possible, the Hanger Charitable Foundation has supported nonprofits such as the Challenged Athletes Foundation and Camp No Limits for children with mobility challenges.

Disaster relief. Disaster relief is a very common, though inherently *reactive* (rather than *proactive*) type of philanthropy. Recent tragedies in the world, such as the Phuket tsunami or the Nepal earthquake, cry out for support.

Some companies make direct monetary donations to relief efforts for the people affected by the disasters. Others offer a vehicle for employees to personally donate and help ensure that the money gets to a reputable aid organization. The most popular form of disaster relief is to match employee donations, creating a bigger overall impact. This type of giving cannot be planned in advance but it enables employees to feel good about their employer as a compassionate business.

Sponsorships. One last, very popular method of giving cash for firms is through sponsorships. In these cases, a business makes a donation at a certain dollar amount, usually to support an event. In exchange, the firm is recognized as a sponsor during the event. Many businesses consider this a form of marketing because they are being recognized directly and publicly for their giving. A classic example is sponsoring a charity golf tournament designed as a fundraiser for the nonprofit. The sponsors are generally promoted on signs at one of the golf holes during the tournament or during the awards ceremony. If the level of donation is high enough, sometimes the donor is announced at the event or even allowed to say a few words. This visibility promotes the firm and connects it to a good cause.

Hahn Texas, mentioned earlier, is a strong advocate of sponsorships as a means not only to directly support great causes, but also to provide the company with favorable visibility both from the event's promotion and through employee attendance at the event.

Donating time: volunteering

The second method of giving back is volunteering, whether together as an employee group or personally by individual employees. It too is a great way to give back. In the aforementioned expression of giving "time, talent, and treasure," volunteering equates to time.

As mentioned in Chapter 2, employees love it when their company supports the community. And volunteering has other benefits as well. According to a UnitedHealth Group study:[70]

- 78% of people who volunteered in the previous year reported lower stress levels

- 76% say that volunteering has made them feel healthier

Laura Arrillaga-Andreesen, in *Giving 2.0*, cites two studies showing that people who volunteer are healthier and happier than those who don't. Other studies are now showing that benefits from volunteering include a longer lifespan, better pain management, reduced stress, and lower blood pressure, with one study citing evidence of a 22% reduction in mortality. And of course the feel-good benefits of volunteering increase personal and organizational health through team building and connections made among colleagues doing good work together. This form of giving ultimately leads to greater happiness in people's lives, creates a more active corporate community identity and sense of pride, and increases work productivity.[71]

Financially, Americans give away around $358 billion every year. Government statistics about the value of volunteering would tell us that $184 billion was donated in 2013, contributing more than half as much as economic donations.[72]

The chart below shows that volunteering is growing yearly and now eclipses pro bono donations:

More Companies Gave Time Off for Volunteering in 2013

Percentage of Companies Offering
Domestic Volunteer Programs by Year

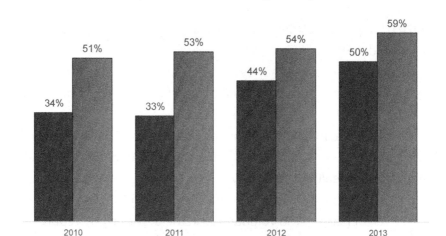

From *Emerging Trends in Corporate Contributions, CECP, https://www.michiganfoundations. org. Reprinted by permission of CECP.*

Almost all companies we spoke with were surprised at how passionate employees are about giving back. Says Gene Austin, ex-CEO of Convio and now President of Bazaarvoice, "There is a tremendous sense of pride among our employees to give back to the community in which they live."

Rocky Epstein, Marketing and Communications Director with the Austin Diagnostic Clinic, says, "After 18 years, I continue to be surprised by the level of generosity exhibited by our physicians and staff. Even during the recent recession, we were able to fulfill requests for fans in the summer or Christmas wishes for children in need. I am fortunate to work with people who care so much about their community."

Encouraging employees to volunteer can take many forms; the benefits derived from volunteering are also varied and can be very helpful to achieving business goals.

Benefits of employee volunteer programs

■ Ranked No. 1 ■ Ranked No. 2 ■ Ranked No. 3

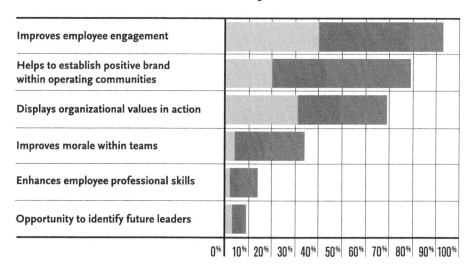

From "Community Involvement Study 2015" ©2015, Boston College Center for Corporate Citizenship. Reproduced with the permission of Boston College Center for Corporate Citizenship.

A somewhat different view of the types of volunteer opportunities comes from the CECP's *Giving in Numbers*:

Corporate Volunteer Opportunities, 2014, Percentage of Companies Offering Each Program

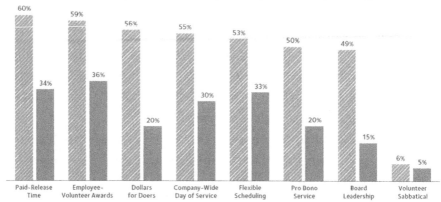

Volunteer Program Offered Domestically   Volunteer Program Offered Internationally
Note: Domestic refers to corporate headquarters country. International refers to all other countries.

From Giving in Numbers, 2014 Edition, p. 23, http://cecp.co/. Reprinted by permission of CECP.

You will notice that most of these categories have been or will be covered in this chapter:

"Days of caring." Employees volunteering as a work group is a very popular option because it leads to enhanced teamwork. People working together to help others puts them outside their usual work environment and allows them to interact in a different setting. As with our personal lives, giving back takes us away from our own problems and enhances our feeling of well-being. So in the workplace, invariably employee groups who volunteer together come back to the workplace transformed and with much closer working relationships with each other.

A supporting study by the UnitedHealth Group found that 81% of people who volunteered agreed that volunteering together strengthens relationships among colleagues.[73]

Many firms find that their employees love "days of caring"-type volunteering:

> For its annual Day of Caring, Hahn Texas chooses a different nonprofit each year so the volunteering benefits are spread more fully throughout the community over time.

> Convio supported "Convio Cares Week" in which teams of employees volunteered for various nonprofits throughout the week.

> The Advisory Board, a nationwide healthcare consulting firm, also has a week of caring each fall with teams going out each day of that week to volunteer with different nonprofits, similar to Convio.

> Plante Moran has a company-wide program called P&M Cares which connects staff to team-based opportunities to help the community. The focus is on giving time or talent rather than money. As an example, the company supported a walk for the March of Dimes in which a team from the company participated in the walk, raising $4,000 for the cause through their efforts. Cincinnati Managing Partner Jim Rolfes says that these types of collaborative volunteering opportunities are great team building activities.

> BuildASign strongly encourages its work teams to volunteer together, either during National Volunteer Week, United Way's Day of Caring, the Entrepreneur Foundation's Service Day, or any other time that works well for that team's work schedule. Team members purposefully plan projects both on- and offsite during working hours, and team members use their "volunteer time off" (VTO) to participate. More than 25% of the staff volunteered during National Volunteer Week alone, but the volunteer projects are conducted throughout the year, especially during the holiday season.

In many communities, the local volunteer center organizes annual days of caring. You may want to align with these initiatives as the nonprofits are prepared for large groups and have specific projects designed for the volunteers.

A note of caution: it is difficult for nonprofits to design a project for your team with very little notice, and a lack of preparation can be frustrating for both sides. So plan ahead and make sure the time spent is valuable for everyone involved.

Personal volunteering. Many companies also encourage their employees to volunteer, allowing them a certain number of hours of paid time off in order to do so. You can see by the chart on page 104 that this is commonly called "paid-release time." As mentioned previously, some firms take it a step further, actually paying the nonprofit an amount per hour for the employee's volunteering. This giving methodology, frequently called "dollars for do-ers," obviously provides the nonprofit with a double benefit: free labor and money to go with it.

➤ The Advisory Board provides its employees up to 10 hours per month of paid time off to volunteer; fully 85% of its Austin staff members volunteer.

➤ CLEAResult had staff at its Portland location who wanted to bring employers together with potential employees from the energy industry. They volunteered to organize a "green conference," bringing qualified candidates together with these employers to help improve employment in the area.

Employees typically love time off to volunteer as it not only makes them feel good about themselves but it also varies their work routine.

Board service for nonprofits. All businesspeople have skills that would be useful for nonprofits at the governance level, either on their board of directors or their board of advisors. Donated time for governance from businesspeople is invaluable to the nonprofit community. The business participants bring a different perspective than their board counterparts from the nonprofit world. This variety of opinions can help the nonprofit's leadership make better decisions on tough issues facing the organization.

Most nonprofit boards are staffed heavily with businesspeople as governance functions are easily found in the business world: organizational leadership skills, financial knowledge, event organization, even meeting planning. An added bonus is that business representatives often bring funding to the nonprofits in which they are involved.

Keystone Search is a good example of a company that strongly encourages its employees to serve on nonprofit boards and, when they do, gives them company time to do this good work.

Cardinal Health takes it even a step further: beyond encouraging board service by its employees, it offers $3,500 grants for which employees can apply on behalf of their nonprofits. The company feels strongly that sharing professional expertise with nonprofits, whether on the board or through other volunteering, is valuable to both parties. And the firm is willing to financially fund some of these nonprofits as well. This is effectively another form of dollars for do-ers, but paid specifically as an additional benefit to the nonprofit having an employee on its board.

Volunteering expertise. Sometimes businesses take the lead and request that an employee who has a certain skill needed by a nonprofit serve as a volunteer, thus utilizing his or her expertise. Usually this request comes with paid time off (during business hours) since it is at the business's request. This type of service blends volunteering with donated service because the skill set is integral to the donation.

➤ Hahn Texas, the public relations firm mentioned earlier, provides this type of support in the form of crisis communications consulting. At times, a nonprofit may find itself in crisis and in need of counsel to navigate the minefield that is public opinion. The Hahn Texas team occasionally provides this highly valuable service as a donation to the nonprofit.

> ➤ Likewise, Centennial, an executive search firm in Cincinnati, Ohio will periodically partner with a nonprofit to provide CEO placement and/or career transition services, another highly valuable skill-based offering.

(This type of skill-based volunteering will be further discussed in the next section under donated service.)

Volunteering after hours. Additionally, some companies have decided that while they cannot support paid time off for volunteering, they still want to encourage their employees to either personally give back to organizations of their choice or to participate in company team volunteer projects during out-of-work hours. This type of giving would not then be considered business philanthropy, but it still promotes the spirit of giving back within their staff.

When I (Debbie) worked at AT&T and we supported a fun run to benefit the Cincinnati Ballet, the company donation was only financial. My workforce at the time was paid hourly, so it was difficult to arrange for any significant amount of paid time off. But we did encourage our staff to turn out for the fun run on a Saturday morning, out of work hours. The donated money was a business gift but the employee participation was personal philanthropy since it was on their own time.

Donating products or services _____

The third kind of gift is donations made from your company that involve either products that you normally sell or services that you provide to clients. Under the "time, talent, and treasure" saying, donated service would be considered talent. These offers are considered "in-kind" or "pro bono" gifts. *Pro bono publico*, usually shortened to pro bono, is a Latin phrase meaning professional work undertaken voluntarily and without payment as a public service. Sometimes these gifts are provided at a heavily discounted rate as opposed to totally free, in which case they would be considered partially-donated goods versus totally pro bono (for free).

These types of gifts are a great way to give because you can actually donate more value than the donation costs you, depending on your profit margin. If, for instance, you normally sell a bundle of lumber for $300 but your wholesale cost is $150, you have only spent $150 out of your pocket but the value to the receiving nonprofit is $300. Your donation is half as costly to you but just as valuable for the nonprofit, assuming they would have purchased the product for full value.

This type of giving needs an important qualifier: the recipient must *need* the product or service you are providing or it is likely not welcome. So donating haircuts to Habitat for Humanity is of no use to them and would likely only result in extra work as they attempt to figure out how to deal with your unwanted gift. On the other hand, Habitat for Humanity would be very grateful to receive donated lumber for direct use in building their homes. And back to the haircuts, they would be enormously useful to Dress for Success, an organization that equips women seeking employment to look their best through clothing, make-overs, and other means.

A great example of how in-kind donations can work well for a business is the Milk + Honey Spa in Austin, Texas. Owner Alissa Bayer knew when she started her business that she wanted to give back to the community. But that can be a real challenge in the early years when a business is not yet profitable. She figured out that what she could give was donated services such as haircuts and manicures. In this way she was able to donate a service on occasion to nonprofits who requested a donation. The nonprofit would usually end up offering the Milk + Honey service (haircut, manicure, etc.) as part of a silent auction where event attendees bid on the item, with the winner providing the money bid to the nonprofit. And Milk + Honey paid out very little incremental expense (nail polish, shampoo, etc.) and instead mostly labor and the use of its facilities. Milk + Honey also allows employees to decide on donations. If one of its staff wants to donate their own time providing spa or salon services, the business donates the facility and spa product and foregoes the associated revenue.

Another example of donated services comes from a hospital in the midwest. This hospital worked with Incite, a cause marketing firm, to promote free lung cancer screenings for veterans during the month of November. The campaign resulted in a significant increase, almost threefold, of patient traffic to the cancer unit. Most importantly, of the 100 veterans screened, 24 cases of previously undiagnosed lung cancer were found, allowing them to receive potentially life-saving treatment.

Many other firms offer donated products or services. Here are some examples:

- **Donated products:**
  - ➤ Chez Zee, an iconic Austin restaurant, regularly hosts events such as fundraisers for various selected nonprofits. It even pays all the costs for a specific event so the nonprofit takes home all the earnings for the night.

  - ➤ Standard Heating discovered that its donations would go further if it gave product since the expense was at their cost rather than at the higher value of the product. And to the nonprofits, the higher amount was what they would save from not having to buy HVAC systems in the marketplace.

  - ➤ BuildASign wanted to welcome home the brother of one of the company principals as he returned from active duty. Since the company makes signs, staffers decided a great gift to the family would be to donate a welcome home banner. The success of that sign (think smiling family faces) led to them deciding they would offer similar signs to any military family welcoming home a loved one. The family does not pay anything for the banner itself, only covering the shipping cost. Little did BuildASign know how popular this offer would become — it has donated over $10 million worth of signage to almost 350,000 military families.

  - ➤ Give Something Back has used its supply chain leverage to buy school supplies at cost, which then all went into back-to-school backpacks for underprivileged (Title 1) kids.

- **Donated services:**
  - ➤ Keystone Search has a staff member who developed an e-newsletter called *Pollen*, which shares information about community happenings, including volunteer opportunities. The recipient list is over 5,000 people, and it has prompted all kinds of volunteers to come forward to help the associated nonprofits. The firm also donates one executive search project annually to the nonprofit community.

  - ➤ Door Number 3 donated videography services to Habitat for Humanity, services which make up its core work as an advertising agency.

  - ➤ Quarterly, Hahn Texas donates its marketing expertise to nonprofits in the form of a messaging workshop for a chosen nonprofit. To date, it has conducted over 40 such workshops to help nonprofits build their image.

  - ➤ UMoveItWeCleanIt has philanthropy at the core of its business model. Employees donate time to equip men and women coming out of incarceration to hold a job in janitorial or custodial cleaning. And they support their clients with all of the things that will enable them to be successful, such as helping them find a job, keep a job, etiquette for employees, etc.

  - ➤ Centennial, an executive search firm from Cincinnati, Ohio, donates executive search capabilities as well as some career transition services each year.

- **Donated resources.** Another great way to donate is to offer the company's *resources* as donations, sometimes neither products nor services. Allowing nonprofits to use company facilities, such as conference rooms for meetings, is an easy way to share. Bulldog Solutions is one company who does this, as does Texas-based Frost Bank.

Milk + Honey does provide a cautionary note: be careful who you affiliate with when donating. An example Alissa, the Founder and Owner, heard about was a marketing firm who donated their services to a "Save Traditional Marriage" campaign. Unfortunately, many of the firm's clients and other constituents were strongly against the campaign and let the firm know it! So do your due diligence before supporting a nonprofit's efforts.

A different form of giving

One last thought about investing. Sometimes one of the best philanthropic investments is right under your nose: helping your own employees in times of need.

Austaco, parent company for over 70 Taco Bell restaurants in Texas, employs mostly low wage earners. These employees occasionally need a little help making ends meet in their daily lives. In one case, an employee's father died out of town and he was terribly concerned about the financial drain of attending the funeral. The Taco Bell where he worked not only gave him time off so he didn't have to forego his wages, but also paid for his expenses to attend the funeral.

This type of benevolence may not be necessary or practical for all companies. But for some companies, an appropriate goal might be to help employees in times of trouble. Needless to say, this business generosity has a hugely positive effect on employee morale and loyalty to the company.

How much to give: financial

Deciding how much to give is a very personal decision, even when the donations are coming from your business coffers. As discussed earlier in this chapter, giving can take three different forms:

1. Financial

2. Volunteering

3. Donated products or services

The most effective philanthropy includes all three types of giving, work-ing synergistically. In this way, a business is less likely, even in lean years, to have to curtail or stop its philanthropy. Even if you might not have the financial means to donate cash in some years, you can still offer some pro bono gifts or volunteers.

Regarding the first category, financial giving, many small businesses have told us that they operate best when they include philanthropy directly in their official budget. There are many ways to decide the right amount:

Percentage. It may help to know the overall business giving percent-ages documented in the following 2015 report from the Committee En-couraging Corporate Philanthropy (CECP), in association with The Con-ference Board:

Year	Total Giving as a % of Revenue	Total Giving as a % of Pre-Tax Profit
2012	0.13%	0.99%
2013	0.14%	0.95%
2014	0.13%	1.00%

From Giving in Numbers, 2015 Edition, p. 23, http://cecp.co/. Reprinted by permission of CECP.

You can see median giving as a percent of either revenue or pre-tax profit to inform the percentage of contributions for your own business.

B-Corporations. Another form of percentage giving has increased dra-matically in recent years. Firms who, as part of their business model, donate a designated percentage of either profits or revenues to phi-lanthropy are springing up in increasing numbers. These businesses are referred to in many states as "for-benefit businesses," an official class of business. In many states they are known as "B corporations."

Give Realty, a real estate firm in Austin, Texas is a great example of this model. Owner Laurie Loew, looking to distinguish herself from the *very* long list of realtors in the marketplace, established her business on the promise of giving 25% of her commissions to the nonprofit of the client's choice. In only eight years, she has donated more than $500,000 to the community. And perhaps as importantly, she is creating new philanthropists as many of her clients have not donated to the community before. This second consequence, seeding the community with new philanthropists, gives her all the gratification that she needs to continue.

Chapter 14 provides more information on for-benefit businesses, but suffice it to say that this method of giving is gaining popularity.

Tithing. The last form of percentage giving is based on the religious concept of tithing. This arbitrary method may make the decision easier. The Christian faith typically advocates tithing or donating 10% of income to charity based on the biblical exhortation in Genesis 28:22: "And this stone, which I have set up for a pillar, shall be God's house. And of all that you give me I will give a full tenth to you."

In Judaism, the obligation to give is called *tzedakah*, meaning "righteousness, justice, or fairness" in Hebrew. For Islam, the practice of *zakat* calls for a certain percentage of income and assets to go to charity. These religions may offer a cut-and-dried way to make this financial giving decision because they provide concrete direction, a percentage, on how much to give.

Set amount. Many others decide on a dollar amount to donate rather than a percentage, and this figure is then a part of the budget — and therefore at least theoretically safe from being reduced or cut out altogether.

Billy Gammon of Gammon Insurance, a Higginbotham company, advocates for this method, saying, "Once it's in the budget you won't miss the money, and you'll end up earning it back."

As far as deciding how much is the right amount, this is a very unique decision for each business. *You* will need to decide what makes the most sense for your company. Typically, businesses in the earlier stages of their lifecycle don't have as many financial resources as they do after they mature. But Keystone Search, mentioned earlier, is a good example of a firm that built philanthropy into the company culture at start-up. Principal Marcia Ballinger tells about differentiating her executive search firm from the competition by all four partners agreeing to give 7% of partner income to charity . . . even in the first year of operation. Non-partner staff also gets an annual allocation to give away as they see fit. So your business does not need to be long-standing in order to give generously.

Also keep in mind that, as mentioned previously, donating products or services allows the company to donate more if valued at its worth versus the actual cost.

Hahn Texas provides a good case-in-point: it provides marketing services for the Austin Marathon and, because it already has skilled employees working for the firm, it only costs employee time — whereas the value of the donation is much higher when valued at what the marathon would have to pay for this service in the open marketplace. So the "set amount" for Hahn Texas in this case is whatever resources it takes to ensure successful marketing and public relations for the marathon.

What to accomplish. So far we have looked at the amount to give from an internal perspective — what the company wants to give. Another way to consider the appropriate amount to give is to decide on the change you want to see happen in the world and fund a significant, achievable effort to make it happen. Then let the amount needed to achieve the goal dictate your giving amount.

As an example, let's say my company feels strongly about eradicating disease in the world. One concrete effort to make tangible progress towards this goal is the use of mosquito nets in Third World homes to protect people — especially children — from mosquito bites, which are known carriers of life-threatening diseases. So you find a nonprofit that is deploying these nets to people in one city this year, and fund that effort. If the cost is $300,000, then that becomes your philanthropic budget for donations and you figure out a way to fund this amount.

Or it could be as simple but meaningful as The University of Texas football team's goal to brighten the day for some kids with cancer at the Dell Children's Medical Center. A proud anonymous donor relates what happened:

"She was so proud of her hat! It was personally signed by two famous University of Texas football players: the quarterback, Colt McCoy, and running back, Fozzy Whittaker.

"It had been a very long year. Having been diagnosed with sickle cell anemia, she was so tired of the never-ending treatments, but worse were the side effects, especially making her hair fall out so that she was now bald. She was sick to death of having everyone stare and gawk at her.

"But today she was proud of her hat. It showed off that two revered football players cared enough about her to come sit with her during her treatment and personally sign her hat. She decided she would even go to school today, though she hadn't been in months.

"The tears in her mom's eyes when she came out of her bedroom, dressed and ready for school in her hat, saying she wanted to attend school that day, was a testament to the impact seemingly little acts of kindness have on the life of someone."

As much as you can. One last methodology for determining how much to give financially comes from BuildASign, mentioned earlier. BuildASign was determined to fulfill its philanthropic mission of positively impacting the communities of its customers, but needed to ensure sufficient funding. In order to self-fund its philanthropic giving, company leaders decided to allocate the margins (above costs) earned on all nonprofits (even though these were already discounted from their regular margins for these nonprofits) to BuildASign's philanthropy fund — which would then, in turn, fund all its philanthropic giving.

This methodology is a very clever way to make sure the company is setting aside money to donate, while not risking giving away so much that it threatens the business's viability: the profit from all its business clients will keep the business financially healthy.

Therefore, the formula for how much to give is variable and dependent on the amount of nonprofit business done in any given year. Because of this, BuildASign has been able to donate over $1 million worth of signage to more than 1,700 nonprofits around the country since 2010.

How much to give: volunteering _____

As mentioned, volunteering is another excellent way to support the community. Similar to financial giving, two main methodologies are typical: a set amount or giving to accomplish a goal.

Set amount. Volunteering during the workday, of course, takes employees off the job, so most companies have a practical limit on how much employee time can be released for volunteer activities. This methodology establishes a set amount of time — for example, three days or 24 hours annually — that each employee is allowed to take as volunteer time-off or paid-release time. In this way the business only allows the amount of time off it feels it can afford.

It is also typical, if not setting a fixed amount, to impose a limit, such as maximum volunteer hours allowed on company time. This helps prevent potential employee abuse of the privilege, as well as avoiding too much overall time employees spend being paid . . . but not working.

What to accomplish. Similar to the financial gifts, a goal is set for what the business wants to achieve and employees are sought who can help accomplish the goal without regard to a specific limitation on volunteer time off. This approach is generally more realistic for large companies with huge workforces over which to spread the employee time off.

Another factor that affects your decision on how much volunteering to support is that you may not truly be funding anything if employees take time to volunteer during the work day, but then end up getting their work done in their off-hours. This situation is particularly prevalent among salaried management-level employees who are paid the same amount no matter how many or how few hours they work.

Differentiated volunteering. In order to make volunteering work for your business, you may also find the need to segment volunteering. For example, group projects or "days of caring" where a work team volunteers together to build teamwork, are funded from the business, but an individual's volunteer projects are done on employee time (out of work hours).

When I (Debbie) managed the in-bound call center for AT&T back in the 90's, where the work was totally dependent on having employees taking calls at their desks and most employees were non-management and thus paid hourly, it was financially more difficult to support volunteering during work hours. Any time we did so, I had to pay incrementally for replacement workers so the call center could accomplish its work. On the other hand, we were able to support some limited volunteering planning effort during the business day while encouraging the actual team volunteering on weekends.

This arrangement is technically not corporate philanthropy, but it was important to AT&T to support the community and we did so with cash donations combined with employee volunteers (albeit on their own time). My employees loved volunteering because it enabled them to give back to the community and have fun with their coworkers in an out-of-work setting.

Add-on gifts. For those companies that have also enhanced volunteering by paying additional monies to a nonprofit based on their employees' volunteer hours (dollars-for-doers), they will need to consider the financial ramifications as they decide on how much volunteering to support. As an example, as mentioned earlier, the Microsoft Store in Austin, Texas pays nonprofits $17 for each hour one of their employees volunteers with a nonprofit. Each volunteer hour will carry additional cost beyond the lost employee time so you might consider limiting volunteering, paying up to only a certain amount annually for each employee's volunteering efforts, so there is a maximum out-of-pocket donation for this type of giving.

Ultimately, the decision on how much volunteering is right for you is similar to the financial one. Consider how much you can afford: the internal method. Or, using an external viewpoint, consider the impact you want to see and fund the volunteer workforce accordingly.

How much to give: donated product or service____

Again, the decision on how much product or service to donate can be made based on the quantity you have available (internal perspective) or fulfilling a need (externally driven).

Available. Soaring Heart Natural Bed, based in Seattle, Washington found it easy to support in-kind donations because its work product provided a natural outlet. First, because the firm was already selling and delivering mattresses, taking away the old mattresses to recycle was an easy gift of in-kind service time that did not require much extra manpower.

As mentioned previously, Tom's Shoes has received tremendous publicity in the past several years by choosing a business model that includes donating a product, a pair of shoes, for each pair that is purchased. This commitment is part of the company's business model so there's an assurance that the resources will be available.

Minneapolis-based Standard Heating was approached by a youth group that sought to renovate an old abandoned railroad property into a coffee shop where the kids could hang out. The group was requesting funding but as they talked, it became clear that the company could not provide the financial resources they wanted. It could, however, provide the HVAC system they would need instead. Bottom line: a win-win by taking the time to understand the project and all the needs involved.

Fulfilling a need. For Soaring Heart Natural Bed, the stuffing used in the manufacturing process made great pillow filler. So the company turned the resource into a gift of in-kind product, along with volunteering. As mentioned before, a team of employees visited the local hospital and helped the young patients build their own pillows. What a wonderful win-win for everyone! The recipients loved the pillows and the staff who participated loved the experience of giving back.

Salesforce provides a great example of giving all three types of resources, and it developed an easy formula for deciding how much to give: 1% of each.

The "1-1-1" model established a giving plan that set aside 1% of the company's equity for philanthropic donations, 1% of employee time for volunteering, and 1% of products or services to be given away to nonprofits.

The company took the concept a step further by creating "Pledge 1%" that helps startups make a similar commitment by assisting them with some of the more technically-challenging aspects of establishing a corporate philanthropy program.

More than 200 companies have already signed up, including Yelp and Optimizely. Pledge 1%'s partner in New York is the Robin Hood Foundation. Suzanne DiBianca, head of Salesforce's foundation, stresses that it's better to set aside the 1% early so that it is institutionalized into the company culture.

"When I talk to start-up founders about doing this, my reasons are: 1) employees are demanding it, 2) corporations should be accountable to all stakeholders, and 3) because it's a great legacy for CEOs who are building a company to create something bigger," DiBianca says.

San Francisco-based Zendesk, for example, has long used volunteering in the Tenderloin area as a way to attract and retain mission-driven employees.[74]

Making the "how much to give" decision can be approached in the suggested ways above. As we have reinforced, it is a very individualized decision for your own business, dependent on factors that are unique to your finance and staffing models.

You can use the following budget worksheet to develop your budget for each type of giving if it is helpful for you:

TOOL #8: Philanthropy Budget Worksheet			
Philanthropy Budget	**Annual**	**Types of Giving**	**Amount**
Financial Giving	☐ % of Pre-Tax Profits: $ OR ☐ % of revenue: $ OR ☐ Set amount: $	☐ Cash ☐ Restricted Gift ☐ Scholarship ☐ Stock ☐ Microloans ☐ Venture Capital ☐ Workplace Giving ☐ Employee match ☐ Benevolence Fund ☐ Disaster Relief ☐ Sponsorship	$ $ $ $ $ $ $ $ $ $ $
Donated Products and Services	☐ Products ☐ Services	☐ List types of goods ☐ List types of services	☐ Value of goods to be given ☐ Value of services to be provided
Volunteerism	☐ # of hours per employee ☐ # of days of caring	☐ Employee volunteerism ☐ Days of caring ☐ Group volunteer projects ☐ Board service ☐ Expertise	☐ # of volunteer hours by employees x $/hr ☐ # of group volunteer projects and equivalent hours x $/hr ☐ # of days of caring and equivalent hours x $/hr

Key points

- Giving can take three main forms:
  - ➤ Financial
  - ➤ Volunteering
  - ➤ Donated products or services

- There are many ways to give within each of the three types of gifts listed above.

- How much to give of each is a decision very specific to your business.

V is for Vet

9

"To give away money is an easy matter and in any man's power. But to decide to whom to give it and how large and when, and for what purpose and how, is neither in every man's power nor an easy matter."

- Aristotle, philosopher and scientist

We have learned about how giving back offers your business many advantages, including building employee skills, boosting employee attraction and retention, increasing revenue and market share, enhancing your business reputation, and improving the community in which you do business. In the preceding chapters, we've discussed how to choose the causes you want to support and how to develop a philanthropy mission statement. We've also learned how to craft a process to guide your philanthropic decison-making, as well as about all the various ways to give back. But a big question remains: how should you choose precisely which organizations should receive your philanthropy?

Who will make the change happen? _____

In 2015, more than 1.5 million tax-exempt organizations of all kinds (various 501(c) subsectors) were registered with the IRS.[75] Determining which of these nonprofits with which to partner can be confusing . . . but it also has very real consequences. If the partnership goes well, both organizations will hopefully benefit tremendously. But if there is a mismatch, or if one side fails to operate with integrity, then both sides may experience great disappointment and possibly negative publicity.

We remember the example of one business we encountered (that will remain nameless) that decided to partner with a well-known local nonprofit. On the surface, there seemed to be a match. The nonprofit was launching an entrepreneurial business and the business owner had expertise in that area. The business owner expected that, along with his financial contribution, he would be asked for assistance with business development, financing mechanisms, and infrastructure support. However, after receiving the financial donation, the nonprofit didn't contact him again. This experience left him feeling both disappointed and underutilized. When he had the opportunity to renew his agreement with the nonprofit, he chose not to do so. Ultimately, he figured out that he had not thoroughly vetted the organization for its needs, nor had he sufficiently clarified his expectations at the outset.

The vetting process — determining which nonprofit organizations to support — assists in determining a good match. First, consider the organizations to which you are already contributing and identify the following:

- Are you satisfied with the relationship that has been built?

- Does it align with your business values?

- Does it align with the issues that you have identified as wanting to impact?

- Does it provide your business with the marketing or volunteer opportunities that you are seeking?

- Is it able to communicate success back to you?

If the answers to those questions are all "yes," then you may want to continue or deepen the relationship.

If you are considering engaging with a new nonprofit, then it is important to conduct due diligence and ensure that it is a credible, effective organization that aligns with your goals. There are several ways for vetting the nonprofits in which you are interested in supporting:

1. **Charitable rating agencies.** The following national organizations rate nonprofits based on a variety of factors:

   - Charity Navigator (http://www.charitynavigator.org/) evaluates 5,500 charities using criteria that includes administrative costs, working capital savings, revenue growth over time, and fundraising efficiency. The organization is now beginning the process of focusing on outcomes.

   - GuideStar (http://www.guidestar.org/) analyzes the income levels and tax forms of more than 1.5 million nonprofits. It also allows users to post reviews about each nonprofit.

   - The Better Business Bureau Wise Giving Alliance (http://www.bbb.org/us/Wise-Giving) offers reports on 1,200 nationally-soliciting charities that include typical fundraising activities. In addition, about 54 of the 113 Better Business Bureaus in the United States and Canada cumulatively produce reports on over 10,000 locally-soliciting charities using the same BBB Charity Standards as the Alliance.

   - CharityWatch (www.charitywatch.org) dives deep to identify how efficiently a charity will use donations to fund programs. CharityWatch states that it exposes nonprofit abuses and advocates for donor interest.

   - Give Well (http://givewell.org) offers what it considers to be evidence-based, thoroughly vetted and underfunded organizations as its "top charities." Its website also offers a "do-it-yourself" evaluation kit that provides a very detailed vetting process tailored to a range of causes, both domestically and internationally.

GIVE Well Vetting Question Example:

Issue: Education

Sample Organizations: Children's Scholarship Fund, KIPP, Teach for America

- *What do you do to improve K-12 education? What is your relationship with the school? Do you work within it or outside it?*

- *What academic literature on education — particularly randomized controlled trials — exists on the type of intervention you are conducting?*

- *Who is targeted by your activities? What are the requirements for participation? In the case of over-subscription, how do you determine who gets in?*

- *Have you collected any systematic data on student satisfaction/retention? How happy are students with the program? What do they wish were improved? How often do they drop out and for what reasons?*

- *Have you tried to assess the impact of your program on later life outcomes, compared to how participants would have done without the program?*

- *How much has been spent on this program? How many students have been served?*

- *How would your activities change if you had more revenue than expected? Less? Would more revenue translate directly into more students served, and up to what point?*

A note about overhead costs: In June 2013, most organizations that evaluate nonprofits, including the first three organizations listed above, released a joint statement encouraging donors to look beyond the costs of what has traditionally been called "administrative overhead" when deciding which groups to support, focusing instead primarily on results and outcomes. "We ask you to pay attention to other factors of nonprofit performance: transparency, governance, leadership, and results," the letter said.

Nonprofit organizations have to have an adequate infrastructure in place to provide effective services and adequate oversight of their programming, and they need to pay the costs for rent and utilities. The percentage assigned to overhead can also be deceiving. For example, in a small nonprofit, the majority of funding may be to support the salaries of staff, which could be considered overhead. However, as part of your due diligence, you do need to assess how much is included in overhead costs. In general, no more than 30% of the overall budget should be assigned to fundraising and overhead costs.

2. **Annual reports.** Almost every nonprofit produces an annual report. Generally, these can be found on an organization's website. These reports should include a financial review, a summary of accomplishments over the last 12 months (demonstrated through both data and stories), and an acknowledgement of major donors. These reports used to be lengthy, but with new technology they are often now brief and full of graphics — and, as a result, are also much easier to digest.

3. **Site visits.** One of the best ways to learn about an organization is to physically visit and meet with the staff and see its facilities. This provides an opportunity to see where the work happens, get a sense from the staff about how inspired they are by their mission, and learn about unique opportunities that your business may find by working in partnership with them.

Characteristics of effective nonprofits _____

When vetting a nonprofit organization, the following are some key characteristics to help you identify if it might be a good match: a clearly-defined
mission, a strong board of directors, good leadership, fiscal responsibility,
and effective programs. A 2011 article in *The Wall Street Journal* also identified these same characteristics to validate when scrutinizing nonprofits.[76]

> **Mission:** Does the organization clearly articulate its mission, vision, and
> values? All nonprofits should have a clearly stated mission. Many non-
> profits also share their vision for the community and the values under
> which they operate. These items should be easily located on the organi-
> zation's website and in its materials. The mission should be the guiding
> force for the decisions that are made within the organization.

> **Governance:** All nonprofit organizations are required to have a board of
> directors. The directors' key roles are to provide policy governance and
> fiscal oversight. Generally, the minimum number of directors is three.
> However, the board should include enough members to ensure that it
> can provide effective guidance and supervision. The names of the mem-
> bers of the board should be readily accessible, as should the by-laws
> that provide structure on how the board operates. The stronger the
> board, generally the more effective the organization.
> Be cautious if:
>
> - The board consists of the minimum number of people, or
>   includes only the executive director and family members
>
> - There are no term limits for board members
>
> - Turnover among board members is high
>
> - Policies and procedures outlined in the by-laws are not fol-
>   lowed
>
> - The board meets less often than quarterly

Strong executive leadership: Just as with a business, core guidance and inspiration for a nonprofit comes from its executive director. The executive director must serve as the balance between guidance from the board and directing the staff who have to carry out the mission through programming. Research the executive directors of organizations with whom you are considering providing support and determine if they will be good partners with your business.

Fiscal responsibility: While nonprofits are not designed to make money, they should be able to demonstrate that revenues, at a minimum, cover expenses and that fiscal policies are in place and followed. A nonprofit should have an annual budget, diversified funding sources, a sustainability plan, and strong fiscal oversight.

Effective programs: Ultimately, the core reason for a nonprofit to exist is to achieve tangible outcomes. Nonprofits should be able to demonstrate that their programming has a positive impact on their organizational goals and the recipients of their actions.

One personal note is that it is easier to vet organizations in which you already have contacts — you will generally have enhanced confidence in the relationship and the information. So don't be afraid to use your network to both gather relevant information and to make the right connections.

In order to create long-term, meaningful, and strategic philanthropy, you will want to partner with nonprofits that align with your values and interests, provide opportunities for your business to meet its philanthropic goals, and can demonstrate outcomes. This true collaboration leads to better progress. As the old African proverb says, "If you want to go fast, go alone. If you want to go far, go with others."

The tools on the following pages are designed to help you methodically and thoroughly vet prospective nonprofit partners:

Key Questions to Ask When Vetting an Organization

Mission:
- What is the organization's mission statement?
- How does it guide your organizational and programming decisions?
- Is there a vision and set of values that guide your work?
- Provide examples of how the mission has been used to make an organizational decision.

Governance:
- Who is on the board of directors?
- How often do they meet?
- Is there a committee structure? If so, what committees meet?
- Are there financial professionals who oversee the budget?
- How do you recruit board members? What are your term limits?
- How do you determine board leadership?

Executive leadership:
- How long have you been doing this work? What drew you to it?
- What unique skills and passions do you bring?
- What is your vision for the organization?
- How do you impart your vision to the staff?
- What are you most proud of achieving?
- What is the most challenging part of the job? How do you address it?
- What do you most need from a business such as mine?

Fiscal responsibility:
- What is your overall budget?
- How has your budget changed over the last five years?
- Does your budget reflect your organization's priorities?
- Who provides the funding?
- How do you plan to diversify your funding, now and in the future?
- What are your greatest financial challenges?
- What are your greatest financial opportunities?

Effective programs:
- What outcomes are you seeking to achieve?
- How do you demonstrate that your programs are effective?
- How do you use data to make decisions about your programming?
- Do you use recognized best practices in your program? If so, what are they?
- What challenges do you have in evaluating your effectiveness? What plans do you have to overcome them?
- What can you tell me about the effectiveness of your programs that the data does not reveal?

TOOL #9: Vetting Tool for Organizations

Organization: _____	MAX SCORE	Your SCORE	Comments
Financial Health	100 pts		
Clear budget	20 pts		
Meets financial goals	20 pts		
Has financial controls in place	20 pts		
Variety of funding sources	20 pts		
Reasonable balance between infrastructure and program	20 pts		
Organizational Purpose	100 pts		
Clear vision and mission	50 pts		
Programs align with vision and mission	50 pts		
Program Outcomes	100 pts		
Demonstrates success	50 pts		
Uses best practices and research	25 pts		
Adjusts programs based on new information	25 pts		
Leadership	100 pts		
Strong executive leadership	40 pts		
Effective and engaged board	40 pts		
Inspired staff	20 pts		
Your Impact	100 pts		
Welcomes support	25 pts		
Will use gift appropriately	25 pts		
Will recognize gift	25 pts		
Makes it easy to give and volunteer	25 pts		

Once you have reviewed an individual organization, you can use the matrix below to compare it with other organizations that you have evaluated in order to determine which one will be the best match for you and your organization.

TOOL #10: Quantitative Vetting Matrix

Date: _____

Decision maker(s): _____

Dates for decisions this year: _____ _____ _____

Criteria	Nonprofit A	Nonprofit B	Nonprofit C
Financial Health (weighted at 20%)	Score (of 100) x .2 =	Score (of 100) x .2 =	Score (of 100) x .2 =
Organizational Purpose (weighted at 10%)	Score (of 100) x .1 =	Score (of 100) x .1 =	Score (of 100) x .1 =
Program Outcomes (weighted at 25%)	Score (of 100) x .25 =	Score (of 100) x .25 =	Score (of 100) x .25 =
Leadership (weighted at 20%)	Score (of 100) x .2 =	Score (of 100) x .2 =	Score (of 100) x .2 =
Your Impact (weighted at 25%)	Score (of 100) x .25 =	Score (of 100) x .25 =	Score (of 100) x .25 =
TOTALS	Sum of the 5 scores above (max. 100 pts)	Sum of the 5 scores above (max. 100 pts)	Sum of the 5 scores above (max. 100 pts)

Subjective comments: _____
_____
_____
_____

Key points _____

- Review the nonprofit organization's mission, board structure, leadership, fiscal health, and programs.

- Determine if the nonprofit meets your standards for being a good partner.

E is for Evaluate

10

> "The most serious mistakes are not being made as a result of wrong answers. The truly dangerous thing is asking the wrong question."
>
> - Peter Drucker, management consultant and author

Earlier in this book we learned about the benefits of philanthropy: employee attraction and retention, employee skill development, better image for your business, increased revenue, and a better community for everyone to live and work. Beside that, many people perceive philanthropy as a mandate for businesses. We know the next step is to select causes you will support and then to craft your philanthropy mission statement. Then you will choose your philanthropy decision process and decide which resources you will give. Following that, you will develop criteria for selecting which organizations will receive your donations. But how will you know when you have been successful?

How will you know it worked? _____

Businesses want their philanthropy endeavors to have a positive and visible impact. Popular books such as *Strategic Giving*, *Money Well Spent*, and *Give Smart* indicate this desire to give effectively. One of the most common frustrations we hear is that business leaders don't always know if their contributions result in making a difference. It is imperative that before embarking on a philanthropic initiative you answer the questions about what precisely

you want to achieve and how you will know if and when you have been successful.

As *The Business of Generosity* reminds us, "We can be satisfied with feeling good about our generosity efforts and never evaluate how much we
are actually doing good. But in the end, generosity is really supposed to be
about doing good."[77]

Evaluating the effectiveness of your business philanthropy can be challenging. It is recommended that businesses use SMART goals to determine
what you want to accomplish with your philanthropy.

In case you are not familiar with SMART goal-
setting, here is a brief summary of this concept.
SMART goals are:
- Specific
- Measurable
- Achievable
- Relevant
- Timely

Specific connotes that goals are clear and not
open to interpretation. If sponsoring an event,
you might want to request data on event
attendance. This number would be determined
by the number of people attending the event
and measured by the nonprofit.

Measurable indicates that goals should be
quantifiable with a very defined formula of
exactly what the measurement is and where
the tracking data will come from. For example,
75% of employees will volunteer at least once
this year as measured by the time reporting
system (which tracks employee time off for
volunteering).

Achievable means that the goal contains a significant degree of difficulty so that it stretches performance, but is not so totally unrealistic as to be demotivating. I (Debbie) once had a regional boss who forced a quota objective onto his entire organization that was, in my opinion and that of my colleagues, absolutely unachievable. He was new to the organization from another function, so it seemed as if he wanted to prove his worth. Unfortunately his whole group knew we had no hope of achieving our quotas, so we were demotivated for the entire year.

Relevant goals are tied to something meaningful to the project or effort. If you are funding scholarships for a kids' summer camp, you might want to know about how satisfied your particular scholarship recipients were (from a customer satisfaction survey). What might not be as relevant is how satisfied the camp counselors were with their employment there.

Timely is intended to make sure that goals are time-bound and not open-ended. So progress toward the goal should be reported with a designated frequency (monthly, quarterly or annually) and the timeframe should be identified upfront (i.e., accomplished by the end of June 2017).

For businesses, philanthropy goals can be set by answering questions in two key areas:

- What do you want to accomplish with your philanthropy for your business?

- What impact do you want your philanthropy to have in the community?

Impact on your own business

What do you want to accomplish for your business through your philanthropic efforts? As previously mentioned, there are many reasons for businesses to engage in philanthropy, but measuring impact can be accomplished by putting systems in place to 1) set goals, and 2) measure progress against them.

- **Financial resources**. Set annual financial investment goals for the business and consider if you also want to ask employees to contribute. Business contributions can be measured by reviewing quarterly financial reports or creating a charter of accounts that specifically tracks philanthropic contributions. Employee contributions can be captured through automatic deductions on paystubs or through surveys.

- **Employee engagement.** If employee engagement is a key goal, then businesses can use timesheets, sign-in sheets, or employee surveys to capture the engagement of employees in volunteer events or other aspects of the philanthropy initiative. For example, you can measure the number of employees or the number of departments that participated in a food drive, or the number of hours employees spent repairing a home. If you want to measure the *impact* of volunteering, the Independent Sector publishes a report on the value of volunteer time, which in 2015 was estimated at $23.56 per hour.[78]

    Increasing engagement can frequently be accomplished by setting up competitions between individuals or departments for employee engagement and then publicly recognizing those that "win." You can use your internal email or a company newsletter to recognize those individuals or teams that are particularly successful.

- **Employee attraction and retention.** As discussed earlier, research tells us that many employees, especially millennials, expect their employer to be philanthropic. The impact of philanthropy on employee attraction and retention can be measured through employee surveys regarding employee morale and engagement with philanthropy initiatives. Similarly, HR professionals can include questions during the hiring process as well as employee exit interviews to assess the importance of philanthropy to specific individuals and how the business's philanthropy initiatives either encouraged them to join the organization or impacted their decision to stay/leave.

- **Communication.** One of the easier things to measure is the number of positive media mentions related to your philanthropic initiatives. Local newspapers and TV stations are often amenable to stories about businesses doing good work in the community. If you can cultivate a relationship with a particular journalist or TV station reporter or producer, then the odds of the story being picked up are increased. However, even sending a simple email notification can often generate some interest from an outlet that is looking for a "good news" story. It is also possible to generate your own publicity by using social media outlets, which can be measured through — for instance — the number of "likes" a post receives on Facebook or the number of retweets on Twitter. Many businesses also choose to have a section on their website devoted to their community engagement. In this section, you can highlight your community partners, communicate your philanthropic goals, and share the volunteer activities of your employees.

Most firms will measure their philanthropy impact themselves or in combination with the nonprofits they support, but there are many methods of measurement, as shown in the following chart:

Companies Use a Variety of Resources for Measurement Activities in Strategic Giving Programs

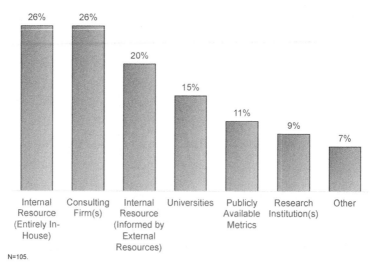

N=105.

From Emerging Trends in Corporate Contributions, *CECP, https://www.michiganfoundations.org. Reprinted by permission of CECP.*

Examples of Evaluation Measures

- Number or percentage of employees engaged in philanthropy program

- Amount donated by business and/or employees

- Number of volunteer hours contributed

- Employee morale

- Employee engagement

- Employees attracted due to philanthropy program

- Employees retained due to philanthropy program

- Number of positive media mentions regarding community involvement

Impact in the community _____

A frequent cause of frustration comes from businesses' inability to quantify the impact their donations have. This usually results from of a lack of strong communication between the business and the recipient organization *prior to the donation*. Both sides should have clear, realistic expectations about the level of accountability. Businesses should remember that nonprofits have to balance their reporting requirements with the size of the gift. Non-profits are generally juggling many different accountability reports. Some basic ways in which you can gather information about the outcome of your contribution is to request information about:

- The impact your contribution made (an end-of-year summary)

- The number of people (if appropriate) impacted by your support

- How your funding was leveraged for additional funding

You can see by the following chart that many companies DO measure the societal value of their contributions:

A Majority of Companies are Measuring the Societal Value of their Contributions

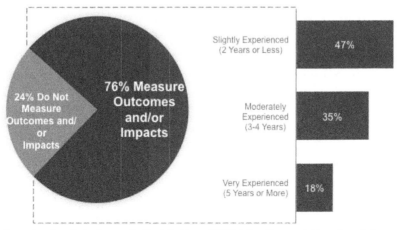

From *Emerging Trends in Corporate Contributions, CECP, https://www.michiganfoundations.org.*
Reprinted by permission of CECP.

And the following chart suggests general ways to consider measuring community involvement success:

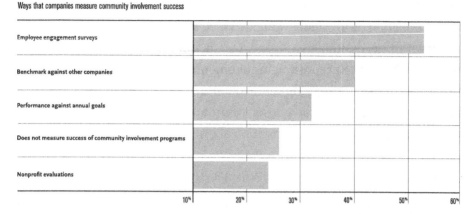

Ways that companies measure community involvement success

Employee engagement surveys					
Benchmark against other companies					
Performance against annual goals					
Does not measure success of community involvement programs					
Nonprofit evaluations					

10%   20%   30%   40%   50%   60%

From "Community Involvement Study 2015" ©2015, Boston College Center for Corporate Citizenship. Reproduced with the permission of Boston College Center for Corporate Citizenship.

As a specific example, Yellow Cab Austin gathers metrics in four areas:

1.   **Money given**
     • Given directly by Yellow Cab
     • Given by personnel who leverage their own donations with a company match

     For example, some employees will organize workplace-based fundraisers for their chosen causes, and the company tracks the total amount raised in this way. In another case, perhaps an employee wants to support his son's robotics team, or a driver wants to buy jerseys for his kid's baseball team, so the company will match money raised for these types of family-oriented activities.

2.   **Hours volunteered**
     • Employee hours given
     • Driver hours given

3. **The experience**

   Yellow Cab surveys participants in the events they sponsor to determine if they enjoyed their experience and whether they would
   recommend that Yellow Cab sponsor it again. This part of the survey is quantitative, but the company also asks for feedback on what
   participants most enjoyed — and, just as significantly, what they
   most disliked — so that Yellow Cab can give this input to the hosting organization.

4. **Impact**

   Yellow Cab also strives to get a sense for the true impact of its donations. A good example of this measurement is funding for Big Brothers Big Sisters (BBBS), where it is known that for every $1,250 donat-
   ed, one child can be mentored for a year by BBBS and its volunteers.
   While this measure is not a true outcome (how the mentored child
   was more successful), funding a child would point towards a positive impact based on BBBS's model.

Yellow Cab is very clear about its reason for measuring its philanthropy:
not to brag about its generosity in an annual report or through media exposure, but rather to continually improve the process, the experience for staff
and drivers, and the impact of its donations. Those metrics are analyzed
annually and used to make appropriate tweaks in Yellow Cab's philanthropy
program so that it gets better year after year.

Similarly, Cardinal Health carefully measures progress towards its philanthropy goals. It has invested significant resources in reducing errors in
the hospital by sharing best practices among constituent partners. This effort has translated into a four-to-one (4:1) return on investment, realizing
$12 million in savings. Cardinal Health's efforts have also resulted in 918 few-
er days in the hospital for patients and — most importantly of all — 14 lives
saved that might have otherwise been lost. For its second philanthropic
goal of addressing prescription drug abuse, the company has developed an
awareness campaign with health professionals to better educate parents,
teens, and the elderly about the causes and dangers of prescription drug
mis-use and theft. The impact on this goal is still being determined.

What to expect from a nonprofit

Businesses should minimally expect to receive a thank-you letter that acknowledges their contribution. If you have made a substantial investment, generally $5,000 or more, a business can request some type of formal impact statement or report. This may include the items above if requested at the time of the donation.

Really good nonprofits will be creative in showing their appreciation. For example, if the donation involved helping children, you may receive thank-you notes from the kids. If you expect some marketing in exchange for your donation, then clarify that expectation. Many nonprofits will list the "benefits" that a business can expect for different levels of donations. If this is not clear, then engage in a conversation with the development director or executive director to make sure that expectations are realistic and can be met. For example, don't expect that you will be designated as a major donor with a $500 gift to a multi-million dollar organization.

Be clear about expectations: prior to making a donation, make sure that you are clear about the expectations you have for what you want to achieve, both internally and with recipient organizations.

What to do with the information

It might take a whole generation to measure the full impact of your efforts, especially if you are involved in education or the environment. As the saying goes, "You don't measure a tree until it has fallen." But that doesn't mean that progress is not occurring or that you should not have interim metrics.

Measuring the outcomes of your efforts should be used to adapt your strategy. You may choose to invest more, less, or not at all depending on the outcomes.

The outcomes can also help you create reports to share with stakeholders about the success of your efforts, further fueling buy-in, resource allocation, and employee engagement.

Key points _____

- Decide how you will measure success with each organization that receives your support.

- Determine how you will measure success for your entire philanthropy plan.

- Clarify expectations with recipient organizations.

- Fulfill your measurement plan — measure the impact!

S is for Start Over

11

"I don't think you ever stop giving. I really don't. I think it's an on-going process. And it's not just about being able to write a check. It's being able to touch somebody's life."

- Oprah Winfrey, talk show host, producer, actress, and philanthropist

Philanthropy, done right, truly is an on-going process. After you have decided what causes to support, crafted your mission statement, chosen your philanthropy decision process, decided what you will give, created vetting criteria for choosing the organizations who will receive your support, developed an evaluation process, implemented your plan and evaluated the impact you had . . . now it is time to "start over."

You don't start over in the literal sense, but rather make new decisions for many of the elements of the philanthropy plan based on new and up-dated information. All of the experience you have had with your current philanthropy should inform what comes next. Some elements may stay the same, but some may change. Elements that tend to stay more constant are causes supported and your overall mission statement. Elements that tend to change include quantities of resources to be given away and which orga-nizations will receive your gifts.

From our personal experience, we have been consistent in our goal of supporting philanthropy in the community but have changed which orga-nizations receive our gifts after evaluating the impact and, in some cases, deciding that the desired results were not achieved. We have also changed the amounts of donations, happily being able to increase support for some over time based on our perception that they were not only good stewards of our gift but were also attaining the expected impact in the community.

Most organizations make this an annual process. On the other hand, if some of your donations are to very long-term projects with results projected only after several years, your annual review in this case will be of progress toward goals rather than necessarily meeting all of the long-term anticipated results.

Create a culture of philanthropy

One other companion imperative for great philanthropy is to proactively build a culture of philanthropy within your organization. This is definitely easier said than done, but there are a few steps you can take to help the process along:

1. **Engage your employees**. Create opportunities for your staff to participate in philanthropy. As mentioned, you can devise group projects for work teams, line up employees with appropriate nonprofit board positions, encourage personnel to volunteer according to their particular personal interests, and even offer paid time off to volunteer. You will find that most of your staff will take advantage of opportunities to give back if you put these in front of them.

2. **Make it personal**. One great way to help your employees get started is to inspire them to service. If they do it once, they will likely want to give back again. Encouraging involvement comes naturally if inspired through storytelling, sharing others' personal experiences with philanthropy and the impact it had on their lives. These stories can be shared in many ways, ideally face-to-face, but also through company newsletters or communiqués, either in writing or — better yet — by video.

3. **Talk about it**. The organization should regularly communicate what it is doing to support the community. Talking about it lets the

employees know that it is an important element of the company's bedrock identity.

4. **Model it**. As with most initiatives, they are most successful when supported from the top. It is therefore important for company leaders to model philanthropic behavior, participating in the community with employee groups or on their own with personally chosen non-profits. In essence, you need to "walk the talk."

5. **Celebrate it.** Celebrating giving back lets your staff know that the organization is serious about its philanthropy. Some companies give out awards to employees who exemplify giving back; lifting them up as positive examples can also do the trick. Any spotlight that is given to philanthropy will tend to reinforce it in your culture.

Integrating philanthropy into your company culture will not only foster momentum for giving back, but will also attract and retain employees who share similar values.

The most important concept of this chapter is to realize that your philanthropy should be an iterative process, to be revisited at regular intervals to ensure maximum impact for your investment. *The Business of Generosity* says it this way, "Generosity is a heuristical practice. As a generosity community, we do something, see what happens, and figure out what to do next at that point. Again and again and again."[79]

Remember the Tom Kochan quote about giving that we shared at the beginning of this book: "It is a virtuous cycle."

Key points

- Revise your philanthropy plan going forward based on learnings from implementing your current plan and evaluating its impact.

- Realize that good philanthropy is a continual process of doing, evaluating, and revising the plan.

Creating Your Philanthropy Plan

12

"No act of kindness, no matter how small, is ever wasted."

- Aesop, author

We hope you have been able to review the previous chapters and identify, for your own business, all of the elements of a successful philanthropy plan:

G = Gear-up: Determine what causes you will support.

I = Identify: Shape the vision for your philanthropy, how you will make decisions about giving back, and what you will give back.

V = Vet: Decide which organizations will receive your support.

E = Evaluate: Measure the impact you have had as a result of your donations.

S = Start over: Finally, use a variety of metrics to iteratively refine your philanthropy plan.

It is important to document your work in a formal philanthropy plan in order to guide your efforts throughout the year. When I (Debbie) ran the philanthropy efforts at AT&T, we had a very organized process that we followed, including a philanthropy team that made resource allocation decisions. I only wish that I had documented our plans so that when I left, I could have more easily turned it over to my successor. Instead, she had to be brought up to speed by the team and did not have the benefit of all the collective wisdom garnered from several years of doing this work.

Businesses know that in order to be successful they need a strong and sustainable business plan. The same is true for creating a strategic philanthropy program. Once you have identified your mission, vision, and goals, it is important to have a formal written document that captures the information, guides strategic philanthropy investments, and assigns responsibility. Your business's philanthropy plan should be used to guide your decision-making, identify who is responsible for follow-through, and outline what you want to achieve. The plan should be evaluated at least annually so that you can determine if you are making progress toward or meeting your goals.

Core components of a written philanthropy plan ___

- **Mission/purpose statement for business philanthropy:** The plan should include your philanthropy mission statement to provide guidance to those accountable for implementing the plan, as well as those making philanthropy decisions. For example: *Laundramutt wants to reduce the number of animals without a home.*

- **The issues for which support will be provided:** Identify the general issues which your business will support. For example: *ABC Medical Clinic will support 1) health awareness and education, and 2) alleviating children in poverty.*

- **Types of organizations to be supported:** State the parameters of the organizations that can be supported. For example: *All donations must go to a registered 501©3 nonprofit organization.* This classification is the most common type of tax-exempt nonprofit organization as its activities have certain purposes — most generally charitable — but can be others such as religious, scientific, etc.

- **How you will give (including how employees will be engaged):** Define if your giving will be in the form of 1) financial, 2) volunteer, or 3) donated (in-kind) products or services. For example: *Charlie Brown Footballs will donate cash, footballs to youth groups, and support employee volunteering through team projects as well as individually.*

- **Annual goals/budget:**
  - ➤ Internal goals: Include annual goals for how much you will give for each type of giving above (financial, volunteer hours, and donated products or services). For example: *XYZ Construction Company will donate a half percent of net profits, allow each employee to volunteer up to 24 hours per year, support one team volunteer day, and donate construction management services for two projects.*

  - ➤ External goals: Identify specific goals for your chosen cause. For example: *Bark and Purr will increase the spay/neuter rate by 20% and decrease the number of shelter days for cats and dogs by 10%.*

- **Specific organizations to whom support will be provided:** Include specific organizations that will be supported by your business (to the extent to which you have made this determination at the time of planning). For example: *Yummy Restaurant will support the Food Bank, Caritas food pantry and Autism Services.*

- **Person/people who will be responsible for the implementation and oversight of the plan:** For any plan to be successful, it is critical that someone, whether an individual or an assigned group of people, is in charge and held accountable for its implementation. For example: *Suzy Supporter will lead the philanthropy team, to be chosen each year with a representative from each of the three geographic regions, one employee from the HR department, and one employee from the marketing department.*

- **Dates for evaluation:** The plan should include regular reviews and a formal evaluation at least once per year. For example: *Rich Accounting Services will review donations annually for the calendar year during year-end reviews done in the first quarter.*

TOOL #11: Sample Business Giving Plan

Business Name:

Mission/purpose statement:

Plan owner(s):

Key issues to support:

Date plan is in effect:

Date plan will be reviewed:

Annual goals/budget:

Organization or issue*	Who will participate?	Type of giving (financial, volunteerism, in-kind)	Frequency of giving (monthly, quarterly, annually, etc.)	Success measures or goals

*Parameters on organizations to be supported (ie. *Organizations must be a 501 (c) 3)*

Signatures of those responsible:

_____

_____

_____

The plan should be visible within the business and presented in a format that is easy to use. It should be a concise document (ideally no more than a dozen pages) to which both leadership and employees can refer when they are making decisions regarding philanthropic investments.

A separate communications plan should be developed that outlines both the internal and external communication plan for sharing your philanthropic success. Guidance about how to do this can be found in the next chapter.

Key points

- Be sure to document all of your work in a formal philanthropy plan.

- Use the tool provided on the preceding page as a starting point, tweaking it as appropriate for your business.

- Set a date for its review.

Telling Your Philanthropy Story

13

"We make a living by what we get, but we make a life by what we give."

- Winston Churchill, British statesman

A s discussed in earlier chapters, there are advantages for both your employees and your business to participating in philanthropy. We know that employees are attracted to businesses that give back, so it is important that they know about all of your good work. We also know that consumers feel businesses should give back to the community, so it is critical that you tell the world about your efforts in order to realize the benefits of enhanced reputation and increased revenue and market share.

Communicating your philanthropy story is a hugely important element of your overall giving effort. While it may be tempting to keep your giving "under the radar," either because you are humble and don't feel you need or want recognition, or because you are afraid you will be buried in a plethora of donation requests, please consider the fact that your philanthropy may provide inspiration or ideas to others about how they might give back to the community.

You have undoubtedly seen the advertisements for Target, Walmart, Amex, Pepsi, and other large corporations that talk about their commitment to giving back and even promoting brands which, when bought, accrue a percent of the revenue to be given to certain causes. You have also probably seen publicity photos in local newspapers or business journals of oversized checks being held up by proud recipients and donors. The *Austin Business Journal* even has a section in each weekly edition with photos of nonprofits' gifts and check presentations.

Boston College's Center for Corporate Citizenship says, "Businesses appear to be recognizing that to link their products and services with an image of responsibility and reap the reputational benefits, they must do a better job of being transparent and telling their corporate citizenship stories."[80]

And, as mentioned before, because consumers are expecting businesses to be good corporate citizens, it stands to reason that they long to hear positive stories about companies who are giving back.

There are two main types of constituents to consider when crafting your philanthropy communication plan:

1. Internal, to those within the company, and

2. External, to those outside the company

Internal philanthropy communication _____

Employees will constitute the largest group of internal constituents, but don't forget about the business partners who collaborate with you in various aspects of developing, manufacturing, distributing, or selling your product or service.

As discussed in earlier chapters, there are numerous benefits to business philanthropy, not the least of which is that employees love to feel proud of the company they have chosen to work for. The Center for Corporate Citizenship reminds us to "embrace the power of your team members as advocates who can bring your message to life and make it their own."[81]

Employees can be the very best mouthpieces to spread the word about all your good work, through word-of-mouth or social media, but you must be sure they know what's going on in order for them to be effective evangelists for your efforts.

Following are some ways to consider telling the story about all of the great work that you are doing to support the community:

- **Newsletters**. Use your company newsletter or e-news to share what's going on with philanthropy in the company.

- **Website**. Be sure to have a section on your website highlighting your community support. Many companies are now posting philanthropy annual reports that share all the good work that has taken place throughout the year. See examples from Hewlett-Packard and REI at:
  - ➤ www.hp.com/us/en/hp-information/global-citizenship/reporting.html
  - ➤ www.rei.com/stewardship/report/2014/stewardship-report.html

- **Meetings**. Share philanthropy stories at leadership and team meetings.

- **Blogs**. If your company has a blog, include philanthropy among the regular business topics, perhaps written by guest bloggers who are directly involved in your company's efforts to give back. You should also consider blogs on general philanthropy to help your staff understand the importance of your giving.

- **New hire orientation**. A perfect time to tell the story about your support of the community is to new hires so they understand, as soon as they come on board, the importance of philanthropy to your company's culture.

- **Philanthropy involvement "cheatsheet."** Make available a "how to get involved" set of instructions to all employees, distributed internally or on the company intranet.

External philanthropy communication _____

You will want to tell your story to those outside the company (not on payroll or a partner) including your customers, your referral sources, industry colleagues, and the community-at-large. In fact, CONE Communications Executive Vice President for Research and Insights, Alison DaSilva, says, "Companies (and nonprofits) really need to do a better job of articulating the impact they're having."[82]

Recent research from the Edelman Trust Barometer shows that 63% of the general population needs messages to be repeated between three and five times to be believed. So a multi-channel approach, including social media, is critical. According to a blog post from Boston College's Corporate Citizenship Center, "Don't ignore digital, and understand the increasing influence of 'search.' When it comes to business information, consumers are increasingly referring to search engines."[83]

Examples of communication methods to your external audience include:

- **Website.** Of course, your website is hopefully viewed by those outside your company and so it should have a section to celebrate your generosity. The number of companies reporting their social and environmental performance has been steadily increasing over the years, and almost two-thirds of large companies now do so.[84] Many businesses have a separate tab or section on their website that is specifically devoted to their community involvement activities.

- **Blogs.** So too, blogs can and should be used to share your philanthropy externally.

- **Public relations.** Using the local media is a great way to tell the story of what you are doing for the community, and most are looking for "feel good" stories. Build relationships with the various types of media outlets — television, print (newspaper, magazines, etc.), radio, and internet — and they will most likely be glad to share your story.

- **Industry relations.** Trade publications or online forums may be another effective way to spread the word about your good work in the community. This sharing can be done both through articles they publish, whether written by you or them, or by paid advertising where you highlight your giving.

- **Social media.** For those of you whose business is on LinkedIn, Twitter, Facebook, Youtube, Instagram, or other social media networks, these avenues are a wonderful way to share your good news and have others share it with their friends and followers for an even broader reach.

- **Point of purchase customer donations.** We all know of retail establishments that give a small percentage of each purchase to a chosen nonprofit. This type of giving makes it obvious to your customers that you are a generous community supporter and good business citizen.

    Some firms such as Give Something Back, mentioned earlier, designate 100% of their profits to go to philanthropy with customer and employee votes choosing the portion that goes to each nonprofit. Other companies offer the ability for customers to donate to a selected cause, usually either by rounding up their charges to the next dollar or by adding a set amount (usually one dollar) to their payment. While this kind of donation is technically not corporate philanthropy because the gift is coming from the customer's pocketbook, the company is still the facilitator of the donation and therefore is viewed favorably as a "giver."

Other ways in which you can share your community involvement include:

- **Marketing collateral.** You are surely proud of your giving. Your employees certainly are too, so what better way to get the word out about your generosity and the causes you care about than to include it in your marketing collateral? This could include items such as brochures, sales proposals, digital information on your website or elsewhere, fact sheets, newsletters, and other customer materials.

- **Sponsorships.** Opportunities abound to sponsor various galas, golf tournaments, and other events that benefit the hosting nonprofit. This can be a very visible way to let event attendees know of your community generosity, especially if participants are either potential customers or can help spread the word about your philanthropy. Sponsorships are almost always structured so that the donating company is promoted as part of the event in exchange for either a cash donation or donated product or service needed for the event.

- **Product donation.** As mentioned earlier, one very popular way for companies to participate in philanthropy is to donate a product that the nonprofit can sell during a silent or live auction at the event. For example, Kendra Scott, a jewelry maker headquartered in Austin, Texas frequently donates a pair of her very popular earrings or other item of jewelry to events to be auctioned off.

- **Advertising.** One sure way to get the word out about your philanthropy is to buy space for an advertisement. You will get the best return on your investment if you determine who you most want to reach and how you can most effectively reach them. This might be trade publications for industry colleagues, either suppliers or customers. Or it might be radio or newspaper (print or online) if you are a retail establishment and want to reach the community at large.

- **Recruiting tools.** Potential employees (along with those who ultimately are hired) are a great audience for your philanthropy story. Tools used to recruit for your business should therefore include a note about your giving. This could include recruiting brochures, company fact sheets, advertisements for employees, and any other recruiting materials.

- **Philanthropy groups.** In some cities, there are organizations dedicated to promote philanthropy. For example, Austin Gives is a program that encourages and recognizes business philanthropy in Austin, Texas. All businesses that donate at least 1% of their pre-tax earnings to philanthropy (including monetary donations, donated products or services, or volunteer hours) are invited to join for free. These "members" are then recognized throughout the year in traditional media, social media, on the website, and at an annual award celebration. Keystone is a similar program in Minneapolis (in fact, it was the role model for Austin Gives) for companies who donate at the 2% level. And other cities like Denver and Bethesda, Maryland have begun similar programs. Be sure to take advantage of these groups because they can help you get the recognition you deserve for your generosity.

The 2013 Cone Study includes data on the most effective communication channels:

Most effective communication channels for information about social and environmental programs and products:

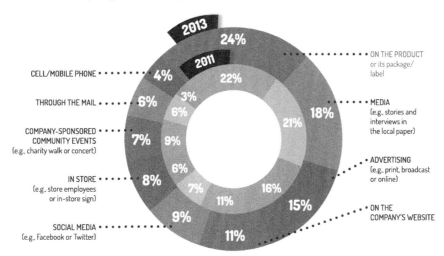

From 2013 Cone Communications / Echo Global CSR Study, http://conecomm.com/. Reprinted by permission of Cone Communications.

You may have other ways to tell your story. Just be sure you do, so you don't lose the benefit, both internally and externally, of your generosity.

Key points

- Consider that sharing your philanthropy story may inspire other firms to take action.

- Make sure your employees and partners know about all of your good work and feel good about sharing it.

- Don't be afraid to tell everyone outside the company too that you are a good corporate citizen. Studies show that consumers want to support givers — you can be sure your suppliers and industry colleagues feel the same way.

Philanthropy Trends 14

"I've always said that the better off you are, the more responsibility you have for helping others. Just as I think it's important to run companies well, with a close eye to the bottom line, I think you have to use your entrepreneurial experience to make corporate philanthropy effective."

- Carlos Slim Helú, Mexican business magnate

As we move into the future, we may see more "kinder capitalism" or "capitalism 2.0" models in which businesses take much greater responsibility for their conduct and impact on society and work actively with governments and civil society to address social challenges both in the United States and globally. To achieve this, traditional philanthropy models will need to look holistically at a company's role and impact on society and change to actively bring its full assets to bear on addressing society's challenges.

Emerging models for corporate giving

Most corporate giving trends relate to businesses aligning with larger community efforts to solve common problems. If companies wish to engage in these efforts, they will have to be willing to put the time into collaborating with other community partners . . . and understand that they are playing a part in the solution for which outcomes may take a while to become evident. This works well for larger businesses that have the time and people power to participate, as well as the desire to be part of larger impact. It may not be as effective for smaller organizations or those that want to see a more immediate impact.

- **Collective impact.** Collective impact has been championed by FSG (Reimagining Social Change), which states that collective impact occurs when organizations from different sectors agree to solve a specific social problem using a common agenda, aligning their efforts, and using common measures of success. These are large efforts with multiple partners focused on problems such as addressing entrenched poverty. For business leaders, this will mean learning how to incorporate their strengths, passions, and values with these other entities, as well as learning to speak and respect each other's languages and ways of working.

- **Pay for Success.** In Pay for Success models (previously called social impact bonds) private funds are used for a daunting array of complex social problems, such as reducing high crime rates in specific areas, alleviating homelessness, and finding more effective ways to deal with chronic disease. Pay for Success projects require government agencies, service providers, and funders to agree on targeted outcomes for a societal issue. Government and project partners then enter into a multi-year contract in which the government agrees to make "success payments" to the private funders if targeted outcomes are achieved. While this is not strictly a philanthropic approach, it is gaining traction as a way to solve complex community problems.

- **Sustainable Value Creation.** From the business vantage point, Sustainable Value Creation has emerged as a self-reinforcing, trustworthy, pro-social corporate behavior model to simultaneously deliver bottom line results and community benefits. Companies following this model will develop a customized strategy tailored to their own business ambitions. The process begins by rigorously selecting social issues on which they lead and engage, taking care that the issues are integral to achieving their businesses goals as well. The key to sustainability is that the effort will create tangible competitive advantage so it becomes a business imperative.

- **Utlilization of technology.** Many businesses are using technology in creative ways to determine their philanthropy areas of focus, engage their employees, and track success. Technology is also being increasingly used to document success stories and consolidate employee giving. New apps are being developed all the time, such as Charity Miles, an application for mobile phones that helps people raise money for charity when they walk, run, or bike. Technology can be an asset in streamlining and tracking your business philanthropy.

Corporate structure

As we formed our philanthropy consulting business, we had to decide on an organizational structure. One of our first decisions was whether to be for-profit or not-for-profit. If we became a nonprofit, we could conceivably qualify for capacity-building and other grants. However, we would have to create a governing board and operate under the other qualifications and constraints of being a nonprofit. We quickly decided that we wanted to be a for-profit consulting business as we desired the flexibility and autonomy that it allowed. However, to support the "nonprofit" ideals we had, we made giving back to the community a core component of our business plan.

We were inspired by the example set by Laurie Loew at Give Realty. As you might remember from an earlier chapter, Laurie started Give Realty after going through a divorce that forced her to re- examine her financial priorities. In her own words:

> *When I was told I would make a good realtor, I wasn't sure if it was a compliment or an insult. In 2005 I ended up getting my license and realized real estate was the career for me! I loved the people and the process. But, to be honest, one of*

the main reasons I was able to enjoy it is because I didn't have to make a living at it. My financial security disappeared in 2007 when I got divorced. After much soul searching and a dollop of Catholic guilt, I decided to create a philanthropic real estate brokerage to differentiate myself in the real estate world. Creating Give Realty is the bravest and most rewarding thing I have ever done.

Give Realty donates 25% of every commission to the 501(c)(3) charitable organization of the client's choice. Between 2008 and 2016, the firm has donated over $500,000 to nonprofit organizations. Give Realty has grown to include seven other realtors who share Laurie's philosophy. Laurie says that one of the things of which she is most proud is that she is creating new philanthropists — for many of her clients, this is the largest check that they have ever been able to give to charity. Laurie is seen as a leader in the social entrepreneurship movement in Central Texas and around the nation and is now frequently called upon to consult with other realtors and individuals interested in social businesses. To learn more about Give Realty and Laurie's philanthropy vision, visit their website: http://www.giverealty.com/.

There has been an increasing trend of creating businesses that have a core component of giving back to the community embedded in their structural DNA, but there is not one term to define them. There are a variety of structures that use various names to describe similar functions, including:

- **Social business.** This term was first defined by Nobel Peace Prize laureate Professor Muhammad Yunus, who described it as "a cause-driven business":

  In a social business, the investors/owners can gradually recoup the money invested, but cannot take any dividend beyond that point. The purpose of the investment is purely to achieve one or more social objectives through the operation of the company, no personal gain is desired by the investors. The company must cover all costs and make profit, at the same time achieve the social objective, such as, healthcare for the poor, housing for the poor, financial services for the poor, nutrition for malnourished children, providing safe drinking water, introducing renewable energy, etc. in a business way.

He further says, "The impact of the business on people or environment, rather than the amount of profit made in a given period, measures the success of social business. Sustainability of the company indicates that it is running as a business. The objective of the company is to achieve social goal(s)."

- **For-benefit corporation.** Similarly, the term "for-benefit corporation" has been defined by the Fourth Sector as organizations that "integrate social and environmental aims with business approaches."[85]

  Attributes of a for-benefit corporation include:

  > *Social purpose:* The for-benefit corporation has a core commitment to social purpose embedded in its organizational structure.

  > *Business method:* The for-benefit corporation can conduct any lawful business activity that is consistent with its social purpose and stakeholder responsibilities.

  > *Inclusive ownership:* The for-benefit corporation equitably distributes ownership rights among its stakeholders in accordance with their contributions.

  > *Stakeholder governance:* The for-benefit corporation shares information and control among stakeholder constituencies as they develop.

  > *Fair compensation.* The for-benefit corporation fairly compensates employees and other stakeholders in proportion to their contributions.

> *Reasonable returns:* The for-benefit corporation rewards investors subject to reasonable limitations that protect the ability of the organization to achieve its mission.

> *Social and environmental responsibility:* The for-benefit corporation is committed to continuously improving its social and environmental performance throughout its stakeholder network.

> *Transparency.* The for-benefit corporation is committed to full and accurate assessment and reporting of its social, environmental, and financial performance and impact.

> *Protected assets.* The for-benefit corporation can merge with and acquire any organization as long as the resulting entity is also a social purpose entity. In the event of dissolution, the assets remain dedicated to social purposes and may not be used for the private gain of any individual beyond reasonable limits on compensation.

The fundamental value proposition of a for-benefit business requires that the organization be able to account for its total impact and performance—financial, social, and environmental. Here are a few examples:

Madcap Coffee Company is a purveyor of high quality specialty coffees and committed to socially responsible business practices. Instead of buying beans indirectly, Madcap established direct relationships with growers in Columbia, El Salvador and elsewhere. Madcap works closely with farmers to improve their crops and offers the farmers a better price since the farmers are providing a higher quality product. Madcap's commitment extends to its local community in Grand Rapids, Michigan, as well. Madcap pays above-average wages, and commits itself to zero waste through an aggressive composting and recycling program.

BioCBD Plus™ delivers not only natural and high quality health supplements but also commits to provide its products to everyone, regardless of their ability to pay. The company's scholarships and donations programs put them in the world of social cause. Their success is measured in lives positively impacted rather than filling the pockets of their executives.

> Brewery Vivant, an artisanal beer-maker, was able to challenge the perception that quality beer must come in bottles rather than cans. They explained to consumers the environmental benefits of cans over bottles (less weight, less energy and lower carbon footprint). This change both helped the environment and reduced Brewery Vivant's operating costs.

- **B-Corporations.** "B Corps" are certified by the nonprofit B Lab to meet rigorous standards of social and environmental performance, accountability, and transparency. Today, there is a growing community of more than 1,100 Certified B Corps from 37 countries and over 120 industries working together toward one unifying goal: to redefine success in business.

    The community of Certified B Corps includes well-known brands like Ben & Jerry's, Patagonia, and Etsy. However, any company can start creating a positive impact. The B Corp movement encompasses a wide variety of firms ranging from public utilities like Green Mountain Power to large, public multinationals like Natura to small tech startups, like Kickstarter.

    And, as the movement grows, it has become an increasingly powerful agent of change. Benefit corporation legislation has been passed in 27 states to create a new corporate form giving business leaders and investors a new freedom to make decisions that are in the best interests of society as well as their bottom lines.[86]

- **Social enterprise.** The Social Enterprise Alliance describes social enterprises as businesses whose primary purpose is the common good. They use the methods and disciplines of business and the power of the marketplace to advance their social, environmental and human justice agendas. There are three characteristics that distinguish a social enterprise from other types of businesses, nonprofits and government agencies:[87]

  > It directly addresses an intractable social need and serves the common good, either through its products and services or through the number of disadvantaged people it employs.

  > Its commercial activity is a strong revenue driver, whether a significant earned income stream within a nonprofit's mixed revenue portfolio, or a for-profit enterprise.

  > The common good is its *primary* purpose, literally "baked into" the organization's DNA, and trumping all others.

Edgar and Joe's restaurant in Canada focuses on building employment skills for underemployed groups, such as at-risk youth or former drug addicts. Profits from sales of food and beverage go to wages, training, and social betterment programs for the staff, helping them learn and grow their skills within the hospitality industry.

Textbooks for Change repurposes used textbooks by providing them to students at underserved universities in the developing world. Profits support social programs in developing communities.

Whatever formal term they use to describe the structure, the reality is that there is a growing movement to pair business with social responsibility. Some entrepreneurs are trying to use a business structure to address a social problem.

One of the most famous examples, previously mentioned, is TOMS Shoes, which began its philanthropy by giving a pair of shoes for every retail pair sold. TOMS has now expanded into eyewear and coffee sales. As of 2015, its philanthropy has provided more than 35 million pairs of new shoes to children in need, helped restore sight to over 250,000 people, and provided a week's worth of clean water for every bag of coffee purchased.[88]

Similarly, Mitscoots partners with local homeless organizations to donate a pair of socks for every pair that is purchased. However, as part of its "Get, Give, Employ" mission, Mitscoots also works with organizations that specialize in taking individuals off the street and hires individuals who are homeless or formerly homeless to package and ship its socks. This approach provides both a meaningful job experience and income to the workers.[89]

In other cases, business owners choose to donate a percentage of their revenue. At Successful Giving, we donate 10% of our pre-tax revenue back to local organizations that help strengthen philanthropy in our community, such as Little Helping Hands (which offers hands-on volunteer opportunities in the Austin community to educate young children about the value of community service) and I Live Here I Give Here (which encourages individual philanthropy through its annual giving day called Amplify Austin).

Other social enterprise models have had similar success. Austin Hospitality was founded in 2008 as a for-profit business to broker and manage overflow business from Austin hotels. In 2010, Austin Hospitality transitioned to Hotels for Hope when hotel partners were asked to make a $1 donation for every actualized room night, which Hotels for Hope then matched, creating a $2 donation to charitable organizations that help children live happier and healthier lives. In 2015, the model evolved with the launch of a new giving platform called RoomFunding™.

This model also allows nonprofits to propose funding for specific children-related projects. The project must fit one of the six focus areas: advocacy, arts, education, health, humanitarian aid, or mentorship. Clients and individuals are then able to apply their room nights to the nonprofit project of their choice; projects are funded based on the number of room nights that are committed.

In 2015, Hotels for Hope was on track to book 80,000+ room nights annually with goals to expand into new meetings and events, create stronger partnerships, and grow staff throughout the United States. With flexible technology platforms and commitment to customer service, Hotels for Hope had already donated in excess of $500,000 using this crowdsourcing approach.[90]

Lessons learned

In the past five years, we have witnessed many well-intentioned individuals forced to move away from their original business intent and either convert to becoming a nonprofit or close their enterprise altogether. Following are some lessons learned for those who are considering venturing into the social enterprise world:

1. **Have a solid business plan.** Just because a business is built on a desire to do good in the world, it will not necessarily succeed as a profitable business. When designing the business it must first be sustainable, with all the financial planning and modeling in place that any other business has to create. We have seen many cases where the focus and passion at the onset was on the philanthropy plan — but a lack of corresponding focus on the core business ultimately resulted in the firms not being profitable enough to sustain themselves. On the other hand, as an example, Grameen has demonstrated over a number of years that their model is financially sound *and* good for the lives of their loanees.

2. **Be the best at your core business.** The reason that companies like TOMS and Mitscoots are so successful is that they have created a

quality product that customers want to purchase. People choose Give Realty and Hotels for Hope because they provide quality services in their field of expertise. While individuals may be initially attracted to using a business because of its social mission, if the product or service is not exemplary, that social mission will not be enough justification for them to continue as customers.

As an example, one company that failed is Cause, a restaurant and bar in Washington, D.C. whose social mission was to dedicate all of its profits to nonprofit organizations. It's an approach that might have worked if the "philanthropub" had been profitable, but sadly it never broke into the black. Cause did succeed in attracting some customers because of its social mission, but it wasn't enough to compensate for the company's confused marketing efforts, founders who were never fully committed to the enterprise, and the host of usual problems that most new restaurants and bars confront. Cause closed after just 14 months in operation.[91]

3. **Don't expect nonprofit organizations to be your primary marketing tool.** Executive directors of nonprofit organizations are often approached by individuals who promise that if the nonprofit supports them, then their organization will receive a financial benefit. You may have heard of this referred to as "cause marketing." One car company I'm familiar with offered a financial incentive to any car buyer if they mentioned Junior Achievement (JA). In these cases, the car dealership would then provide JA a stipend for each car sold, incentivizing JA to market this program to their many supporters. However, as in any other enterprise, these nonprofit executives have to weigh the cost/benefit analysis and often will not be willing to promote a social enterprise until they can determine that it is demonstrably viable and will have a direct impact on their bottom line. In the case of JA, no cars were sold under the program, resulting in a substantial resource drain with no payoff.

Whatever term or structure you use to describe your business, the important thing is that you focus on issues that are meaningful to your business and employees, and then be good at whatever you do. The more successful your business is, the greater opportunity you will have to give back.

Key points

- There are numerous new business models that incorporate social impact as part of the business's fabric.

- Be the best at your core business and have a sustainable business model.

- Don't rely on nonprofits to market your business.

Conclusion 15

"I think the great livers, the people who are fully self-actualizing and alive, are the great givers."

- Mark Victor Hansen, motivational speaker, trainer, and author

Over the course of this book, we hope that you have learned much about business philanthropy, and that you realize some of the benefits of giving back:

Internal:
- Improve employee attraction and retention
- Enhance employee skills

External:
- Build brand and reputation
- Increase revenue and market share

Moral:
- Improve the community
- Altruism — it is the right thing to do

We also hope you have been able to work through the various aspects of a successful philanthropy plan and have documented one for your own business:

G = Gear-up: Determine what causes you will support.

I = Identify: Shape the vision for your philanthropy, how you will make decisions about giving back, and what you will give back.

V = Vet: Decide which organizations will receive your support.

E = Evaluate: Measure the impact you have had as a result of your donations.

S = Start over: Finally, use a variety of metrics to iteratively refine your philanthropy plan.

Making philanthropy a priority _____

There is much to indicate that good corporate citizenship seems to be on the upswing in priority for businesses — to truly aim to not only make money, but also to make the world a better place. Research done by Boston College noted that a company moves through various phases in its journey of corporate citizenship, from fairly simple philanthropy to more complex and sophisticated initiatives.

**DEVELOPMENTAL CHALLENGES THAT TRIGGER
MOVEMENT OF CORPORATE CITIZENSHIP**

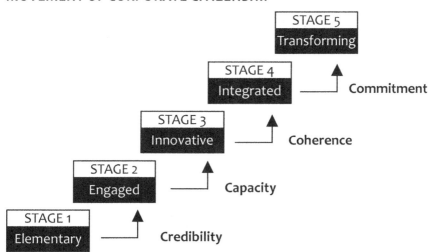

From Stages of Corporate Citizenship: A Developmental Framework by Philip Mirvis, Ph.D. and Bradley K. Googins, Ph.D., ©2006, Boston College Center for Corporate Citizenship. Reproduced with the permission of Boston College Center for Corporate Citizenship

The study found that businesses tend to be ahead in some dimensions and behind on others, meaning that they are not purely in one stage at a given point in time. But they do tend to move up the chain toward the upper right as they establish their credibility, build their capacity, synergize their efforts, and then integrate their commitment to corporate citizenship into their business strategies and culture.

In the first stage, **Elementary**, citizenship activity is episodic and programs are generally undeveloped. In stage two, **Engaged**, companies move toward embracing social responsibility rather than just complying or doing good now and then. For the third stage, **Innovative**, the social responsibility agenda becomes more comprehensive and the company assumes more of a stewardship role. The fourth stage, **Integrated**, sees companies progressing from coordination to true collaboration, and citizenship is driven throughout the lines of business, often including executive-level citizenship resources. Lastly, in stage five, **Transforming**, the companies are out front, innovating and leading (rather than imitating) and they view themselves as global citizens — they take their role in philanthropy very seriously.

Unilever is a good example of a company at the Transforming stage. Its goal was to help the poor in underdeveloped countries in two ways:

1. Address a dietary deficiency with iodized salt

2. Reduce diarrheal disease through enhanced hand washing

In both cases, the company devised new supply chains to make its products available to the very poor via new distribution channels. This effort has since spread into water purification and children's nutrition. While Unilever is obviously very large and therefore has access to significant resources, small businesses can similarly have great impact if properly mobilized.

Mike Duke, ex-Walmart CEO, sums it up best: "More will be expected from market leaders and globally successful companies and those companies who are most involved will be most successful, creating an upward spiral."[92]

We believe business philanthropy is here to stay. Most business owners feel it's just the right thing to do. Others recognize that there are practical reasons such as increased revenue, enhanced employee skills, improved brand strength. Some want to support the community to ensure a better place to live for all citizens. And our younger generations are fairly insistent on working for companies which are good corporate citizens, both environmentally and societally. Clearly employees, consumers and business owners all feel that philanthropy is a good thing.

We hope you will take some of the tips in this book and the many lessons shared to build your own successful philanthropy plan. Your company will be better for it. Your employees will love you for it. And the world will be a better place for it. Let's all subscribe to Tom Kochan's belief that "it is a virtuous cycle" and make it an integral part of our how we conduct our business.

Once again, we hope you will give for **good** — helping the world become a better place to live, as well as give *for good* — investing in the community for the rest of your life!

References

1. Giving USA, "Giving USA Annual Report," 2015, www.givingusareports.org

2. The Case Foundation, "Inspiring the Next Generation Workforce: The 2014 Millennial Impact Report," 2014, http://casefoundation.org/wp-content/uploads/2014/11/MillennialImpactReport-2014.pdf

3. The Conference Board, "Report Offers Recommendations to Boards of Directors for Ensuring Effectiveness of Corporate Giving Programs," *Director Notes*, August 2, 2011

4. Bruce DeBoskey, "Seven Steps towards Strategic Corporate Philanthropy", *Denver Post*, March 7, 2015

5. Sandra Larsen, "The Business Case for Corporate Philanthropy", Accessed June 30, 2009, www.sandra-larson-consulting.com/articles/The-Business-Case-for-Corporate-Philanthropy

6. Laura Quinn and Jessica Baltes, "Leadership and the Triple Bottom Line", Center for Creative Leadership ©, 2007

7. Global CSR Study, *Cone Communications/Echo*, 2013, www.conecomm.com/global-csr-study

8. Mike Spector, "What Can Individual Donors Learn from Corporate Philanthropy?" *The Wallet, Wall Street Journal*, February 25, 2009

9. "The New Paradigm: Volunteerism. Competence. Results." *Forbes/Insights,* © Forbes 2011

10. Trend Watching, "Generation G," February 2009, Accessed February 27, 2016 http://trendwatching.com/trends/generationg/

11. Bentley University, "Millennials in the Workplace," www.bentley.edu/centers/center-for-women-and-business/millennials-workplace

12. Bob Murphy, "Why Making an Impact is Good for Recruitment, Retention and Production," *Triple Pundit,* April 1, 2015

13. Stephanie Vozza, "Why Every Company Should Pay Employees to Volunteer," *Fast Company,* March 11, 2014

14. David Bruce Montgomery and Catherine Ramus, "CSR Reputation Effects on MBA Job Choice" (working paper), Stanford University Graduate School of Business, 2003, http://www.gsb.stanford.edu/faculty-research/working-papers/corporate-social-responsibility-reputation-effects-mba-job-choice

15. Stephanie Vozza, "Why Every Company Should Pay Employees to Volunteer," *Fast Company,* March 11, 2014

16. Sandra Larsen, "The Business Case for Corporate Philanthropy," Accessed June 30, 2009, www.sandra-larson-consulting.com/articles/The-Business-Case-for-Corporate-Philanthropy

17. Carolyn Cavicchio, "Building the Business Case for Cause-related Marketing," February 27, 2004, Accessed June 30, 2009, www.convio.com

18. *Cone/Roper Cause Related Trends Report,* 1999, Cone, Inc. and Roper Starch Worldwide

19. Grant Thornton LLP and Business Week Research Services, "Corporate Responsibility: Burden or Opportunity," *Business Week,* © 2007

20. The Case Foundation, "Inspiring the Next Generation Workforce: The 2014 Millennial Impact Report," 2014, http://casefoundation.org/wp-content/uploads/2014/11/MillennialImpactReport-2014.pdf

21. Suzanne Lucas, *CBS News Money Watch*, November 12, 2012

22. Susan Cramm, "Strengthening Your Cultural Fortess," *Strategy + Business blog*, June 23, 2015

23. Stephanie Vozza, "Why Every Company Should Pay Employees to Volunteer," *Fast Company*, March 11, 2014

24. Sandra Larsen, "The Business Case for Corporate Philanthropy," Accessed June 30, 2009, www.sandra-larson-consulting.com/articles/The-Business-Case-for-Corporate-Philanthropy

25. D.A. Jones, "Does Serving the Community Also Serve the Company? Using Organizational Identification and Social Exchange Theories to Understand Employee Responses to Volunteerism Programme," *Journal of Occupational and Organizational Psychology*, 83 (4), 857-878, 2010

26. "The New Paradigm: Volunteerism. Competence. Results." *Forbes/ Insights*, © Forbes 2011

27. Sandra Larsen, "The Business Case for Corporate Philanthropy", Accessed June 30, 2009, www.sandra-larson-consulting.com/articles/The-Business-Case-for-Corporate-Philanthropy

28. "Young People's Volunteering and Skills Development," *The National Youth Agency, Department for Education and Skills, Research Report RW 103* [no date]

29. Deloitte/Point of Light, *Volunteer IMPACT Study Executive Summary*, page 3, 2006

30. Stephanie Vozza, "Why Every Company Should Pay Employees to Volunteer," *Fast Company*, March 11, 2014

31. Dr. Christine Carter, "What We Get When We Give," *Greater Good Science Center*, 2010

32. Adam Pickering, "Giving makes us happy: charity improves well-being for donors too," *Future World Giving*, March 20, 2015, www.futureworldgiving.org

33. Mirco Tonin, Michael Vlassopoulos, "Note to bosses: workers perform better if you give to charity," The Conversation, January 7, 2015, http://theconversation.com/note-to-bosses-workers-perform-better-if-you-give-to-charity-35873

34. Mirco Tonin, Michael Vlassopoulos, "Corporate Philanthropy and Productivity: Evidence from an Online Real Effort Experiment," *University of Southhampton*, CESifo working paper series no. 4778, April 27, 2014

35. Adam Pickering, "Giving makes us happy: charity improves well-being for donors too," *Future World Giving*, March 20, 2015, www.futureworldgiving.org

36. Stephanie Vozza, "Why Every Company Should Pay Employees to Volunteer," *Fast Company*, March 11, 2014

37. Stephanie Vozza, "Why Every Company Should Pay Employees to Volunteer," *Fast Company*, March 11, 2014

38. Philip Mirvis and Bradley Googins, "What Drives Companies to Embrace Corporate Citizenship," *Stages of Corporate Citizenship: A Developmental Framework*, 2006, page 16, The Center for Corporate Citizenship at Boston College Monograph

39. The Conference Board, "Report Offers Recommendations to Boards of Directors for Ensuring Effectiveness of Corporate Giving Programs," Director Notes, August 2, 2011, accessed August 4, 2011, www.conference-board.org/directornotes

40. "The New Paradigm: Volunteerism. Competence. Results." *Forbes/ Insights*, © Forbes 2011

41. Gladys Edmunds, "4 Strategies for cost-conscious marketing," *USA TODAY*, July 9, 2009

42. Stephen Graves, *The Business of Generosity*, page 45

43. Kristi Oloffson, "In Toms' Shoes: Start-Ups Copy 'One-for-One' Model," *Wall Street Journal*, September 30, 2010

44. "The Global, Socially-conscious Consumer," *A Nielsen Report*, March 2012, www.bostoncollegecorporatecitizenship.org

45. "The New Paradigm: Volunteerism. Competence. Results." *Forbes/ Insights*, © Forbes 2011

46. Anna Pivosky Auerbach, "Making Customer-driven Philanthropy Work," Stanford Social Innovation Review blog, April 20, 2015, http://ssir.org/articles/entry/making_customer_driven_philanthropy_work

47. Ed deHaan, "How to Rebuild Trust after a Scandal," *Stanford Graduate School of Business*, January 14, 2014, http://www.gsb.stanford.edu/insights/ed-dehaan-how-rebuild-trust-after-scandal

48. Raymund Flandez. "Most Consumers Who Buy Charity-Linked Products Want Results," *Chronicle of Philanthropy*, October 2, 2013

49. Robert P. McNamara, "A New Era of Sustainability UN Global Compact," *Accenture CEO Study*, 2010, U.S. Environmental Protection Agency – Product to Service Transition

50. Gene Epstein, "Charity Has Its Rewards for Generous Companies," *Wall Street Journal*, January 7, 2007

51. "The New Paradigm: Volunteerism. Competence. Results." *Forbes/Insights*, © Forbes 2011

52. Katherine V. Smith. "From the Corner office: perspectives on corporate citizenship," *Corporate Citizenship* blog, June 8, 2015, Boston College Center for Corporate Citizenship, http://corporatecitizenship.bc.edu/from-the-corner-office-perspectives-on-corporate-citizenship

53. Stephen Graves, *The Business of Generosity*, page 61

54. Stephanie Vozza, "Why Every Company Should Pay Employees to Volunteer," *Fast Company*, March 11, 2014

55. Howard Schultz, "Invest in Communities to Advance Capitalism," Harvard Business Review blog, June 30, 2015, https://hbr.org/2011/10/ceos-should-invest-in-communit

56. *State of Corporate Citizenship in the United States*, 2009, The Hitachi Foundation and the Boston College Center for Corporate Citizenship, page 43

57. John F. Kennedy and Bill Adler. *Uncommon Wisdom of John F. Kennedy: A Portrait in His Own Words*, 2003

58. Dotson Rader, "Growing Good Citizens," *Parade Magazine*, March 29, 2015

59. Millennium Report Toronto: *Environics*, 1999: 2003, referencing *Stages of Corporate Citizenship in the U.S. 2006*, The Center for Corporate Citizenship at Boston College by Philip Mirvis and Bradley K. Googins

60. Mark Horoszowski, "7 Research-backed Ways Your Business Will Benefit by Being More Socially Responsible," *Huffington Post What's Working: Purpose + Profit*, June 30, 2015 by, as quoted from the *Harvard Business Review* by Michael Porter and Mark Kramer

61. The Conference Board, "Report Offers Recommendations to Boards of Directors for Ensuring Effectiveness of Corporate Giving Programs," *Director Notes*, August 2, 2011, accessed August 4, 2011, www.conference-board.org/directornotes

62. Stephen Graves, *The Business of Generosity*, page 38

63. The Conference Board, "Report Offers Recommendations to Boards of Directors for Ensuring Effectiveness of Corporate Giving Programs," *Director Notes*, August 2, 2011, accessed August 4, 2011, www.conference-board.org/directornotes

64. Stephen Graves, *The Business of Generosity*, page 38

65. Anna Pivosky Auerbach, "Building a Culture of Philanthropy," Stanford Social Innovation Review blog, September 19, 2014, http://ssir.org/articles/entry/building_a_culture_of_philanthropy

66. Katherine V. Smith. "From the Corner office: perspectives on corporate citizenship," *Corporate Citizenship blog*, June 8, 2015, Boston College Center for Corporate Citizenship, http://corporatecitizenship.bc.edu/from-the-corner-office-perspectives-on-corporate-citizenship

67. Ed deHaan, "How to Rebuild Trust after a Scandal," *Stanford Graduate School of Business*, January 14, 2014, http://public-prod-acquia.gsb.stanford.edu/news/headlines/ed-dehaan-how-rebuild-trust-after-scandal

68. Dan Graham, "Here are the five worst pieces of advice you'll ever hear," *Austin Business Journal*, April 10, 2015

69. *Emerging Trends in Corporate Contributions*, Committee Encouraging Corporate Philanthropy (CECP), https://www.michiganfoundations.org Permission by CECP.

70. United Health Group. *Doing Good is Good for You: Health and Volunteering Study*, 2013

71. Dr. Christine Carter, "What We Get When We Give," *Greater Good Science Center*, 2010

72. *Giving USA Report*, 2015, www.volunteeringinamerica.gov

73. United Health Group. *Doing Good is Good for You: Health and Volunteering Study*, 2013

74. Kim-Mai Cutler, "Salesforce Expands its "Pledge 1%" Philanthropic Model to New York Tech Companies," posted May 14, 2015, www.techcrunch.com

75. Number of Nonprofit Organizations in the United States, 2003 – 2013, NCCS Business Master File, Accessed September 20, 2015, http://nccsweb. urban.org/PubApps/profile1.php?state=US

76. Emily Grazer, "Dig Deeper When Checking Out Smaller Charities," *Austin American Statesman* reprint of *The Wall Street Journal*, October 30, 2011

77. Stephen Graves, *The Business of Generosity*, page 99

78. "The Value of Volunteer Time," The Independent Sector, 2016, Accessed 09/20/2016, https://www.independentsector.org/volunteer_time

79. Stephen Graves, *The Business of Generosity*, page 108

80. *State of Corporate Citizenship in the United States, 2009,* The Hitachi Foundation and the Boston College Center for Corporate Citizenship, page 26

81. Megan McLaughlin, "CSR professionals share experience in managing internal communication issues," Corporate Citizenship blog, October 22, 2013, Boston College Center for Corporate Citizenship, http://corporatecitizenship.bc.edu/blog/2013/10/csr-professionals-share-experience-in-managing-internal-communication-issues

82. Raymund Flandez. "Most Consumers Who Buy Charity-Linked Products Want Results," *Chronicle of Philanthropy,* October 2, 2013

83. Patricia MacKenzie, "Effective CSR communication: Which tactic when?" *Corporate Citizenship blog,* June 30, 2015, Boston College Center for Corporate Citizenship, http://corporatecitizenship.bc.edu/csr-communication-tactics

84. *State of Corporate Citizenship in the United States, 2009,* The Hitachi Foundation and the Boston College Center for Corporate Citizenship, page 22

85. For-Benefit Corporations, 2016, Accessed July 30, 2016, www.fourthsector.net/learn/for-benefit-corporations

86. Katie Kerr, "Using Business as a Force for Good: The Key to a Better Tomorrow," Skoll World Forum, December 17, 2014, www.skollworldforum.org

87. Social Enterprise Alliance, "Social Enterprise: What's a Social Enterprise," 2009, Accessed January 16, 2016, http://www.northminsterchurch.net/wp-content/uploads/2011/03/2014-01-30-What-is-Social-Enterprise.pdf

88. "Toms Improving Lives: One for On," 2016, Accessed March 19, 2016, http://www.toms.com/improving-lives

89. Mitscoots Outfitters, 2016, Accessed February 26, 2016, http://www.mitscoots.com/pages/faqs

90. Hotels for Hope, 2016, Accessed February 26, 2016, http://www.hotelsforhope.com/giving-back/

91. Eric Nee, "Learning from Failure," *Stanford Social Innovation Review*, February 18, 2015, http://ssir.org/articles/entry/learning_from_failure

92. "Solving Social Problems through Business Strategy," *Shaping the Future: Pathways to Sustainable Value Creation in 2020*, CECP 2010, page 17

1200 Barton Creek Blvd. #7, Austin TX 78735   512 · 517 · 9485
info@successfulgiving.com   www.successfulgiving.com

Dear Reader,

We are so happy you've chosen to spend some time with us on the topic of business philanthropy.

If you are interested in further information and supporting this community, we would love to have you:

1. Review this book at https://www.amazon.com/dp/098639730X/

2. Connect with us on social media at
   - LinkedIn: https://www.linkedin.com/company/successful-giving
   - Twitter: @GoodBizGiving
   - Facebook: https://www.facebook.com/SuccessfulGiving/

3. Contact us at info@successfulgiving.com.

Thanks so much!

Our very best,

Debbie Johnson and Sam Woollard

Made in the USA
Coppell, TX
29 December 2023

27049794R00115